How to Use This Book

Look for these special features in this book:

SIDEBARS, **CHARTS**, **GRAPHS**, and original **MAPS** expand your understanding of what's being discussed—and also make useful sources for classroom reports.

FAQs answer common **F**requently **A**sked **Q**uestions about people, places, and things.

WOW FACTORS offer "Who knew?" facts to keep you thinking.

TRAVEL GUIDE gives you tips on exploring the state—either in person or right from your chair!

PROJECT ROOM provides fun ideas for school assignments and incredible research projects. Plus, there's a guide to primary sources—what they are and how to cite them.

Please note: All statistics are as up-to-date as possible at the time of publication. Population data is taken from the 2010 census.

Consultants: Robert M. Hordon, PhD, Associate Professor, Rutgers University; William Loren Katz; James Lewis, Librarian, The Charles F. Cummings New Jersey Information Center, Newark Public Library; Raymond Frey, PhD, Professor of History, Centenary College

Book production by The Design Lab

Library of Congress Cataloging-in-Publication Data
Kent, Deborah.
 New Jersey / by Deborah Kent. — Revised edition.
  pages cm. — (America, the beautiful. Third series)
 Includes bibliographical references and index.
 ISBN 978-0-531-24894-2 (lib. bdg.)
 1. New Jersey—Juvenile literature. I. Title.
 F134.3.K465 2014
 974.9—dc23   2013032829

©2014, 2008 Scholastic.
All rights reserved. Published in 2014 by Children's Press, an imprint of Scholastic Inc.
Printed in the United States of America 141
SCHOLASTIC, CHILDREN'S PRESS, and associated logos are trademarks and/or registered trademarks of Scholastic Inc.

1 2 3 4 5 6 7 8 9 10 R 23 22 21 20 19 18 17 16 15 14

AMERICA ★ THE ★ BEAUTIFUL

New Jersey

BY DEBORAH KENT

Third Series, Revised Edition

Children's Press®
A Division of Scholastic Inc.
New York ★ Toronto ★ London ★ Auckland ★ Sydney
Mexico City ★ New Delhi ★ Hong Kong
Danbury, Connecticut

CONTENTS

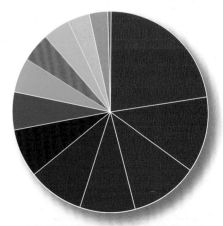

NEW YORK

Delaware

Delaware Water Gap

Kittatinny Mountains

Great Valley

Lambert Castle

PATERSON

Passaic Falls

PASSAIC

Hudson

George Washington Bridge

NEW YORK

PHILLIPSBURG

PENNSYLVANIA

Great Swamp

Raritan

NEWARK

ELIZABETH

Liberty State Park

New Jersey Turnpike

PERTH AMBOY

Sandy Hook Lighthouse

Princeton University

PRINCETON

LONG BRANCH

★ TRENTON

NEW JERSEY

Hadrosaurus Sculpture

New Jersey Shore

CAMDEN

Barrier Islands

ATLANTIC OCEAN

The Pinelands

Pine Barrens

MARYLAND

DELAWARE

VINELAND

Atlantic City Boardwalk

Lucy the Elephant

MARGATE CITY

ATLANTIC CITY

N
W · E
S

Delaware Bay

Cape May

Cape May

0   20
Miles

QUICK FACTS

State capital: Trenton
Largest city: Newark
Total area: 8,721 square miles (22,588 sq km)
Highest point: High Point, 1,803 feet (550 m) above sea level
Lowest point: Sea level along Atlantic Ocean

Welcome to New Jersey!

HOW DID NEW JERSEY GET ITS NAME?

The first people who lived in what is now known as New Jersey called it Lenape-Hoking, or "land of the Lenape people." Later, the first Europeans to land on New Jersey's shores thought they had found an island. The English Duke of York called it New Jersey, after the island of Jersey that lies in the English Channel.

New Jersey is not an island, but it is surrounded by water on three sides. It is joined to the mainland only by a 50-mile (81-kilometer) stretch of land in its northwestern corner. But the state was named for the island of Jersey nonetheless!

NEW JERSEY

READ ABOUT

The Kittatinny
Mountains tower
over the Delaware
Water Gap in
New Jersey, near
the border with
Pennsylvania.

CHAPTER ONE

LAND

★

MORE THAN 200 YEARS AGO, NEW ENGLANDERS NICKNAMED NEW JERSEY "THE GARDEN STATE" FOR ITS RICH, PRODUCTIVE FARMLAND. For generations, fruits and vegetables from New Jersey's farms fed the hungry people in the cities on the East Coast. In its 8,721 square miles (22,587 square km), you'll discover bustling cities, wooded hills and pine forests, deep lakes and lonely marshes. From its highest point at High Point, which is 1,803 feet (550 meters), to its lowest point at sea level, the Garden State truly is a place of beautiful landscapes.

IN THE BEGINNING

During the past two million years, what is now New Jersey lay beneath a **glacier** during three separate periods. The most recent glacial advance (called the Wisconsin) started about 80,000 years ago. It began to recede about 20,000 years ago when it reached central New Jersey. Large amounts of sand, clay, and boulders were deposited on upland areas. Lowlands were filled with up to 350 feet (107 m) of sand and gravel.

The glacier carved out many of the lakes that sparkle in northern New Jersey. Lake Hopatcong, Budd Lake, Green Pond, and Greenwood Lake (which lies partly in New York) were all created by the glacier.

The rocky debris that the glacier left behind formed hills and ridges. One example is a series of cliffs called the Palisades, towering above the Hudson River. West of the Palisades cliffs are the Watchung Hills and the Ramapo Mountains. These were not formed from glaciers but are made of very old and resistant rocks. The Kittatinny Ridge lies along the northwestern part of the state and stretches for 36 miles (58 km). High Point, the highest peak in the state, stands in New Jersey's northwestern corner.

WORD TO KNOW

glacier *a slowly moving sheet of ice*

New Jersey Geo-Facts

Along with the state's geographical highlights, this chart ranks New Jersey's land, water, and total area compared to all other states.

Total area; rank	8,721 square miles (22,588 sq km); 47th
Land; rank	7,417 square miles (19,210 sq km); 46th
Water; rank	1,304 square miles (3,377 sq km); 27th
Inland water; rank	396 square miles (1,026 sq km); 38th
Coastal waters; rank	401 square miles (1,039 sq km); 14th
Territorial waters; rank	507 square miles (1,313 sq km); 13th
Geographic center	Mercer County, 5 miles (8 km) southeast of Trenton
Latitude	38° 55′ N to 41° 21′ 23″ N
Longitude	73° 53′ 39″ W to 75° 35′ W
Highest point	High Point, 1,803 feet (550 m)
Lowest point	Sea level along Atlantic Ocean
Largest city	Newark
Longest river	Raritan, 75 miles (121 km)

Source: U.S. Census Bureau, 2010 census

Among the 50 states, New Jersey ranks 47th in size. It could fit into the state of Texas 37 times.

It is easy to tell where the glacier stopped. It left a clearly marked line that runs across the state west to east, from Phillipsburg to Perth Amboy. Above this line, the land is wrinkled with hills, ridges, and valleys. About two-thirds of the state lies below the line. In this part of New Jersey, the land suddenly becomes smooth and flat.

During the Ice Age, the Wisconsin Glacier helped carve out New Jersey's diverse landscape. Today, you can view the Hudson River from the Palisades Cliffs of New Jersey.

GEORGE INNESS: CELEBRATING THE LAND

As a boy growing up in Newark, George Inness (1825–1894) dreamed of becoming a painter. His father was horrified and tried to distract him by putting him to work in a grocery store. George hid his paints and canvases behind the counter and kept his customers waiting while he painted. When he finally lost his job, his father let him study art. Today, Inness is regarded as one of the finest American painters of the 19th century. He spent the last decades of his life in Montclair, painting the woods and hills near his home.

? Want to know more? Visit www.factsfornow .scholastic.com and enter the keywords **New Jersey**.

New Jersey Topography

Use the color-coded elevation chart to see on the map New Jersey's high points (dark red to orange) and low points (green to dark green). Elevation is measured as the distance above or below sea level.

Elevation	
Feet	Meters
1,100	335
900	274
700	213
500	152
300	91
100	30

LAND REGIONS

New Jersey lies in the mid-Atlantic region of the United States. The Atlantic Ocean laps its eastern shore. The Delaware River and Delaware Bay separate New Jersey from two of its neighbors, Pennsylvania and Delaware, to the west and south. New Jerseyans (sometimes called New Jerseyites) look north to New York across New

Jersey City's Promenade has a breathtaking southeastern view of the Manhattan skyline.

York Bay and the Hudson River. New Jersey would be an island if it weren't for a 50-mile (81-km) boundary with New York at its northwest corner.

New Jersey is divided into four regions: the Atlantic Coastal Plain, the Piedmont, the New England Upland, and the Appalachian Ridge and Valley Region.

The Atlantic Coastal Plain

The flat portion of New Jersey is part of a long, narrow region called the Atlantic Coastal Plain. This region stretches from New England to the Gulf Coast states. New Jersey's richest farmland lies within the coastal

Atlantic City is located along the southeastern coast of New Jersey on one of the state's barrier islands.

WORD TO KNOW

barrier islands *islands that are created by the gradual buildup of sand and stones from the ocean floor*

FAQ

Q8 HOW DID THE PINE BARRENS GET ITS NAME?

A8 Early European settlers could not use the dry, acidic, sandy soil of the Pinelands for farming. From their point of view, the land was barren and unproductive.

plain. The deep fertile soil is easy to farm because it has few stones.

New Jersey has 127 miles (204 km) of coastline, and residents nearly always refer to their Atlantic coast as "the shore." From Manasquan south to Cape May, the New Jersey shore is a tangle of shallow rivers, inlets, sandbars, and barrier islands. Among the barrier islands are Long Beach, Brigantine, and Absecon. Barnegat Bay, a finger of the ocean, separates many of the **barrier islands** from the mainland.

If you travel inland from the New Jersey shore, you will soon reach a region of salt marshes, bogs, and forests of scrub pine, oak, and cedar. This is the Pinelands, sometimes known as the Pine Barrens. The

Pinelands is the largest area of undeveloped land between Boston and Washington, D.C. It covers approximately 22 percent of New Jersey's total area. Altogether the Pinelands contains 1.1 million acres (445,000 hectares) of land.

Beneath the dry, sandy soil of the Pinelands are deposits of sand and clay. The Kirkwood-Cohansey formation consists of sand that holds a remarkable amount of freshwater, estimated at 17 trillion gallons (64 trillion liters).

The Piedmont

To the northeast of the Atlantic Coastal Plain is the Piedmont. About 20 miles (32 km) wide, this area covers only about one-fifth of the state. The major rivers of the state—Hudson, Passaic, Raritan, and Ramapo—are in this area. The Hudson empties into New York Bay and then into the Atlantic Ocean. At the city of Paterson, the Passaic River crashes over a precipice in the Watchung Mountains. It tumbles 77 feet (23 m) into a steep-sided gorge, or canyon. The Raritan River has several tributaries, including the North Branch, South Branch, and Millstone River. These rivers help support the industrial cities of Newark, Paterson, Jersey City, and Elizabeth.

MINI-BIO

SAM PATCH: THE JERSEY JUMPER

On September 30, 1827, crowds gathered at the Passaic Falls. A young Paterson mill worker named Sam Patch (1807–1829) had made a bet that he could jump over the mighty Passaic Falls. As the breathless crowd watched, Patch took an astonishing leap from the riverbank. He soared over the falls and landed unharmed in the foaming water below. His amazing feat earned him the nickname "the Jersey Jumper." For the next two years, Patch toured the country, making daredevil plunges from cliffs and bridges. But one of his jumps finally cost him his life. Patch died in an attempt to leap over the Upper Falls of the Genesee River in Rochester, New York.

? Want to know more? Visit www.factsfornow.scholastic.com and enter the keywords **New Jersey**.

Passaic Falls is the second-highest waterfall in the United States east of the Mississippi. Only Niagara Falls is higher.

Here's a view of the Delaware Water Gap located within the Kittatinny Mountain range.

LAKE HOPATCONG

The largest lake wholly within New Jersey's borders is Lake Hopatcong. It spreads over 4.2 square miles (10.8 sq km) and has 35 miles (56 km) of shoreline. The lake was formed when several ancient glacial lakes combined thousands of years ago. In addition to its glacial lakes, New Jersey has several human-made lakes and ponds. The largest of these is the Wanaque Reservoir, 6.6 miles (11 km) in length. It was constructed during the 1920s and provides water for 85 New Jersey towns.

The New England Upland

This region is sometimes called the Highlands, and it lies west of the Piedmont. There are stunning lakes in the area, as well as flat-topped ridges of rock. The region extends into Pennsylvania and New York.

Appalachian Ridge and Valley Region

This is a mountainous region in the northwest corner of the state. It includes the Kittatinny Mountains near New Jersey's northwestern border. In that same area,

THE HADDONFIELD HADROSAURUS

On a summer night in 1858, a farmer named William Estaugh Hopkins was having dinner with a neighbor at his home near Haddonfield in Camden County. Hopkins showed his neighbor some strange bones that he had found in a **marl** pit on his land. The neighbor, William Parker Foulke, had a keen interest in science. Foulke asked to dig around Cooper's Creek, which was on Hopkins's land. Imagine his excitement when, after two days of digging, he unearthed the bones of a gigantic ancient beast! Although the head was missing, the bones were the most complete skeleton of a dinosaur that had ever been found up to that time. The creature was a plant-eating reptile that measured 30 feet (9 m) long from head to tail. It was named *Hadrosaurus foulkii*. The first part of the name is a combination of the Greek words *hadros* and *saurus*, meaning large or bulky lizard. The second part honors the discoverer, William Foulke.

the Delaware River has carved a deep gorge. The Delaware Water Gap, as this gorge is called, measures 4,500 feet (1,372 m) across at the top. The walls plunge 1,200 feet (366 m) to the rushing river below. There the gap narrows to only 900 feet (274 m) wide. The Delaware River cuts through the Kittatinny range at the Delaware Water Gap. There are many dairy farms and apple orchards in this region.

CLIMATE

New Jersey lies in the Moist Continental Climate Zone. The state can have extreme temperatures. Its winters can be very cold, and its summers can be broiling hot! The hilly northwestern part of the state has the coldest winters and the coolest summers. Winters tend to be gentler in the south. During the summer, cool ocean breezes fan the shore, luring vacationers from inland towns and cities.

Each year, fierce tropical storms brew in the southern Atlantic. Many of them whirl north along the coast. When the winds of a tropical storm reach a steady speed of 74 miles (119 km) per hour, the storm is classified as a hurricane. Tropical Storm Floyd lashed New Jersey in September 1999. Floyd swept away beach

WORD TO KNOW

marl *type of clay containing lime in the form of fossil shells*

SEE IT HERE!

HACKENSACK MEADOWLANDS

In the valley of the Hackensack River is a sprawling, vast saltwater marsh called the Hackensack Meadowlands. Journalist Robert Sullivan marveled that the Meadowlands is "a 32-square-mile [83-sq-km] wilderness . . . that is 5 miles [8 km] from the Empire State Building and a little bit bigger than Manhattan." Beneath the marsh lies an oozing bed of clay and mud up to 300 feet (91 m) deep!

Since the 19th century, the Meadowlands has been used as a dump for factory waste. In the 1960s, however, a portion of the Meadowlands was set aside as a nature preserve.

Hurricane Sandy caused serious flooding along New Jersey's coast in 2012.

cottages, flooded streams and rivers, and washed out bridges. It was the costliest storm in the state's history at the time. However, an even bigger storm hit New Jersey 13 years later. In October 2012, Hurricane Sandy slammed into the East Coast and devastated large parts of the region. In New Jersey, 37 people were killed and about 350,000 homes were destroyed or damaged. Nearly 2.4 million homes were left without power. Damage was estimated at more than $30 billion.

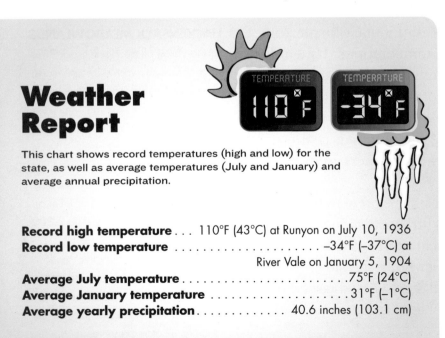

Weather Report

TEMPERATURE 110°F

TEMPERATURE -34°F

This chart shows record temperatures (high and low) for the state, as well as average temperatures (July and January) and average annual precipitation.

Record high temperature . . . 110°F (43°C) at Runyon on July 10, 1936
Record low temperature . . . . −34°F (−37°C) at River Vale on January 5, 1904
Average July temperature . . . . .75°F (24°C)
Average January temperature . . . . .31°F (−1°C)
Average yearly precipitation . . . . 40.6 inches (103.1 cm)

Source: National Climatic Data Center, NESDIS, NOAA, U.S. Department of Commerce

New Jersey National Park Areas

This map shows some of New Jersey's national parks, monuments, preserves, and other areas protected by the National Park Service.

Middle Delaware NSR

NEW YORK

Delaware

Appalachian NST

Delaware Water Gap NRA

Hudson

Edison NHS

Passaic

Morristown NHP

Newark

NEW YORK

Phillipsburg

Elizabeth

Raritan

Edison

PENNSYLVANIA

New Brunswick

Lower New York Bay

Princeton

SANDY HOOK

Gateway NRA

Freehold

Long Branch

Asbury Park

Trenton

0   20 Miles
0   20 Kilometers

N
W   E
S

Camden

ATLANTIC OCEAN

Great Egg Harbor SRR

Vineland

Atlantic City

DELAWARE

Ocean City

Delaware Bay

	National Park area
NHP	National Historic Park
NHS	National Historic Site
NRA	National Recreation Area
NST	National Scenic Trail
NSR	National Scenic River
SRR	Scenic and Recreational River

ANIMAL LIFE

Although New Jersey is a small state, it is home to a remarkable number of animal species. According to the New Jersey Audubon Society, about 500 species of reptiles, amphibians, birds, and mammals live in the state. In late March and early April, the piping chorus of spring peepers signals the end of winter. Bullfrogs,

An Eastern painted turtle

DON'T FEED THE BEARS!

New Jersey's black bear population has risen steadily since the 1970s. Bears in New Jersey have learned to live close to humans, and humans are learning to live close to bears. The New Jersey Division of Fish and Wildlife warns against feeding bears or allowing them access to garbage. Bear attacks on humans are very rare.

green frogs, painted turtles, spotted turtles, and the eastern snapping turtle jump or swim in the lakes and ponds of northern New Jersey. The green turtle, hawksbill turtle, and several other sea turtle species can sometimes be sighted in coves and inlets along the shore. The eastern garter snake is common in suburban and forested areas.

Every fall, bird watchers gather at Cape May to watch thousands of hawks, vultures, bald eagles, and other raptors, or birds of prey, pass overhead as they fly south. Island Beach State Park is an excellent spot to observe migrating shorebirds. About 210 species of birds nest in New Jersey each year, from eagles and owls to sparrows, warblers, and hummingbirds.

New Jersey's deer population increased dramatically late in the 20th century. As more homes were built, animals such as wolves and mountain lions were forced out of the state. But the deer remained and now have no natural predators. In some places, people consider the deer to be pests because they graze on lawns and gardens. Other mammals found in New Jersey include the muskrat, red fox, gray fox, coyote, otter, raccoon, skunk, and opossum. Several kinds of whales cruise along the shore, and seals and dolphins occasionally appear off Cape May and in Delaware Bay.

The lakes and reservoirs of northern New Jersey are full of freshwater fish, including largemouth bass, pickerel, and catfish. Among the saltwater fish found along the shore are bluefish, flounder, mackerel, and striped bass.

PLANT LIFE

Hardwood trees such as the oak, maple, beech, and dogwood flourish in the woods of northern New Jersey. Evergreens are most plentiful along the shore and—of course—in the Pinelands. In some parts of the Pinelands, small pygmy pines grow to be only 11 feet (3 m) tall. The Pinelands is also home to rare orchids that cling to tree branches.

A wide variety of wildflowers bloom throughout New Jersey in spring and summer. Daisies, violets, and buttercups brighten the fields. If you're lucky, you might find a lady slipper or bloodroot. In marshy areas, you may stumble upon the skunk cabbage and jack-in-the-pulpit. A tall, hardy reed called phragmites forms thick clumps along the edges of streams, rivers, and ponds. Phragmites is one of the few plants that manages to thrive in severely polluted areas. When this fast-growing reed takes over, it's a sign that the area is polluted and is in trouble!

ENDANGERED SPECIES

New Jersey is home to some wonderful animals. But some of these animals are endangered. That means that they are at risk of dying out. Among them are the peregrine falcon and the red-shouldered hawk. Endangered reptiles include the Atlantic loggerhead turtle and the timber rattlesnake. Have you ever seen a whale up close? They are remarkable animals! Those endangered along the New Jersey coast are the humpback whale, the fin whale, and the blue whale. Conservation groups in the state are working hard to preserve the homes of these animals and protect them for years to come.

A dogwood blossom

A team of scientists working on a radioactive waste area in Wayne, New Jersey.

WORD TO KNOW

radioactive *giving off atomic particles, which can be dangerous to living things*

CLEANING UP NEW JERSEY

From 1915 to 1926, the U.S. Radium Corporation had a busy factory in the town of Orange in Essex County. The company processed a **radioactive** mineral called radium, used for making watch faces. The factory threw its waste into nearby garbage dumps. Many years later, construction crews leveled the dumps to make room for new houses. Waste from the dumps was mixed in with the soil around the houses' foundations. Eventually, people discovered that 240 homes in Orange had radioactive foundations and stood on dangerous radioactive sites.

During the 1970s and 1980s, the American public became concerned about pollution. The federal government investigated polluted sites all over the country. It turned out that New Jersey, small though it is, had more polluted sites than any other state!

In 1980, the U.S. government set aside money in a special treasury called the Superfund. This money was to be used for cleaning up polluted sites all over the country. Some 9,000 sites in New Jersey were found to need Superfund cleanup. The federal government and the state of New Jersey are working together to decrease pollution. The job is slow and costly, but little by little, it's getting done.

In Orange, the cleanup began in 1997. It was not finished until 2004. Cleanup crews shipped much of the contaminated soil to a burial site deep underground in the Utah desert.

Throughout the state, houses are sprouting up where trees and wildflowers once grew. But New Jerseyans have worked to preserve many of the state's remaining natural areas. New Jersey has 30 state parks, 11 state forests, five recreation areas, and five state marinas. At their many parks, New Jerseyans can watch wild birds and animals in their natural surroundings. New Jersey's natural areas are among the many highlights of the Garden State.

The most popular birding competition in the United States is the one-day World Series of Birding, which is held in New Jersey every May.

THE RADIUM GIRLS

During Word War I (1914–1918), the U.S. Radium Corporation in Orange employed about 70 women to paint watch faces and dial numbers with radium. Radium was used because it glows in the dark. Scientists at the factory used masks, shields, and tongs when they handled this dangerous substance. The women who worked in the factory were not given protective equipment, and were not told that contact with radium was hazardous. After months of work, many of the women got sick. They suffered from bone fractures and anemia (a low red-blood-cell count). When they found out the truth, some of the women sued the company. In the end, they only received $10,000 each. Some died before collecting any money.

24

READ ABOUT

Longhouses were common structures for the Lenni-Lenape people.

c. 10,000 BCE
The first humans reach present-day New Jersey

▲ 500 BCE–500 CE
Ancient people use tools that are later discovered at Abbott Farm

c. 1000 CE
People in New Jersey learn to make pottery

CHAPTER TWO

FIRST PEOPLE

★

THE FIRST PEOPLE IN WHAT IS NOW NEW JERSEY WERE THE DESCENDANTS OF GROUPS THAT CROSSED A HUGE LAND BRIDGE FROM ASIA INTO WHAT IS NOW ALASKA. Little by little, they spread across the continent. Ancient peoples camped on the shore of the Atlantic to fish and gather oysters. Archaeologists know this from sites they have discovered at Island Beach and Toms River.

c. 1200
*The Lenape enter
New Jersey*

1500s
*The Lenape live in
longhouses*

▲**1524**
*Giovanni da Verrazzano's
ship is seen off the New
Jersey coast*

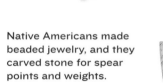

Native Americans made beaded jewelry, and they carved stone for spear points and weights.

The first humans reached present-day New Jersey 12,000 years ago. Most archaeologists believe that they came as the Wisconsin Glacier was receding.

TOOLS AND POTTERY

As the centuries passed, the early people learned to make stone tools. They chipped ax heads out of stone, which they used for chopping down trees. They made thin knives, which they may have traded with other peoples. Because they were often on the move, they didn't accumulate many possessions. But they liked beautiful things, just as people do today. From rare, colorful stones, such as serpentine and rose quartz, they carved beads and pendants. Some stones were carved into the shapes of birds and butterflies. Banner stones were flat carved stones, often in a butterfly shape, with a hole through the middle. No one knows for sure what these stones were for. Some archaeologists think the stones were used as weights on spear-throwing tools called *atlatls*.

At first, the ancient people cooked in wooden or stone pots that they half buried in the ground. The cook built a fire and heated a large stone in the coals. When the stone was very hot, the cook fished it out with tongs and dropped it into the pot full of food. The hot stone cooked the food in the pot.

Around 1000 CE, people in the area learned to make pottery. With clay from the riverbanks, they shaped bowls, pots, and jars. They decorated their pottery with pictures of animals and plants.

SEE IT HERE!

ABBOTT FARM

Abbott Farm, the home of **archaeologist** Charles Conrad Abbott, stands on the Delaware River near Trenton. Abbott found thousands of ancient stone tools here during the late 19th century. Some of his discoveries date from 500 BCE to 500 CE, which is known as the Middle Woodland Period. Today, lectures and exhibits at Abbott Farm teach the public about New Jersey's earliest known inhabitants.

WORD TO KNOW

archaeologist *a person who studies the remains of past human societies*

Examples of Native American pottery, along with knives made of stone and bone

Native American Peoples
(Before European Contact)

This map shows the general area of Native American people before European settlers arrived.

THE ORIGINAL PEOPLE

By about 1200 CE, a new group of people came to the area. They called themselves the Lenape, or Lenni-Lenape. In the Lenape language, the name means "original people."

The Lenape belong to the Algonquin family, a large confederation of Native American groups. The Algonquin lived in eastern Canada and the northeastern United States. They spoke many different but related languages, and they shared some customs and beliefs. Other Algonquin groups respected the Lenape. They were known as "the grandfathers" and were admired for their wisdom. At times, the Lenape were asked to **mediate** in disputes between other Indians.

WORD TO KNOW

mediate *help opposing sides reach an agreement*

The Lenape people were known mostly for their mobility as a hunter-gatherer society, spreading far and wide across New York, New Jersey, and Delaware.

The Lenape lived in both longhouses (right) and wigwams (left).

Q3 WHAT KIND OF HOUSES DID THE LENAPE LIVE IN?

A3 During summer months, the Lenape often lived in wigwams, or they lived in tents made of animal skins. They lived in longhouses, which are long dome-shaped buildings, during the winter.

The territory of the Lenape included parts of New York, Pennsylvania, and Delaware and all of New Jersey. The Lenape divided themselves along political lines into two groups, the Unami and the Munsee. Each group had a separate chief and a council of advisers. The two groups also spoke different dialects. Different subgroups formed from these two main groups. Importantly, a Lenape's social, cultural, and political life was shaped by his or her connection to the tribe, rather than where they lived or the dialect they spoke.

By the 1500s, the Lenape lived in longhouses made of bark during the cold months of the year. They lashed tree branches into place with vines or bark strips to make the frame. They covered this frame with sheets of bark or mats woven of reeds. Towards the south, the Lenape usually lived in single-family houses. Farther north, several related families often lived together in longhouses.

THE LENAPE WAY OF LIFE

Like New Jerseyans today, the early Lenape often went to the shore in the summer. All summer, they fished and gathered clams and oysters. In some places, they left great heaps of oyster shells where they camped year after year.

The Lenape had a varied diet, especially in summer. Women planted corn, squash, and beans. Women and children gathered nuts, berries, and fruit. Wild chestnuts were very plentiful. They would head into the woods with a group of friends and fill sacks full of rattling chestnuts. The men hunted deer, bears, squirrels, rabbits, and many other animals.

No part of an animal went to waste. After the meat was eaten, bones were carved into sewing needles. **Sinews** served as thread. Deerskin made soft, sturdy moccasins, and furs were sewn into winter cloaks.

Lenape women wore long skirts made of skins. Men wore breechcloths, fastened around the waist with a belt. Sometimes the Lenape decorated their clothes with beads and shells. Men often carried their belongings in a beaded skin pouch, slung over the shoulder by a long strap.

Following a network of trails, the early Lenape traveled throughout New Jersey. They visited neighboring groups to share news and to trade. Sometimes, **wampum belts** served as money.

Picture Yourself . . .

Living as a Lenape in the 1500s

Imagine that you are a Lenape growing up in northern New Jersey in the 1500s. You live in a longhouse with your mother and father, your grandparents, an aunt and uncle, and several cousins. At night, everyone gathers inside and sits close to the fire. The wind howls like the call of the wolf, but inside you are warm and safe.

You listen to the crackle of burning branches, and you watch the flames leap and dance. Your mother scrapes a deerskin to make you a new pair of moccasins. You hear the light "chip! chip!" as your father carves an arrowhead from a piece of flint. Your grandfather clears his throat. He begins to tell an old story about a bear hunt when he was a boy. He was tracking a big bear that would provide plenty of meat for the village. He says the bear turned and chased him all the way home. You've heard the story before, but you like hearing it again. Snug in your house with your family around you, you think of the adventures that await you in the forest outside.

WORDS TO KNOW

sinews *tendons of an animal that can be used as cord or thread*

wampum belts *belts that were made by stringing together many round, flat seashells*

SEE IT HERE!

THE WOODRUFF MUSEUM OF INDIAN ARTIFACTS

At the Woodruff Museum of Indian Artifacts in Bridgeton, you can get a glimpse into Lenape life before the arrival of Europeans. On display are Lenape tools, arrowheads, masks, drums, and pots. The museum's collection of some 30,000 objects helps us to learn about the state's early history.

Q8 HOW DID THE LENAPE GET AROUND?

A8 The Lenape traveled on rivers and streams in dugout canoes. Canoes were made from hollowed tree trunks. They also traveled on foot.

LENAPE FUN AND GAMES

The Lenape enjoyed playing games. Some games involved dice carved from deer antlers. In a game called *mamandin*, players shook up several dice in a bowl. The dice were marked with painted spots. The Lenape used notched sticks to keep score.

Snow snake was a great game for midwinter. The players dug a long, sloping trough in the snow and sprinkled it with water. The water froze, making a slick, icy runway. The "snow snake" was a slender stick about 7 feet (2 m) long. Players took turns sending the snake down the trough. The person who managed to send the snake the farthest won.

The Lenape played rough-and-tumble sports and had a game a lot like modern football. Their football game, called *pahsaheman*, was a contest between men and women. Players moved a ball from one end of a field to the goalpost at the other end, just as they do in American football today. But in Lenape football, women could carry the ball in their hands, and men could use only their feet.

SPIRITUAL BELIEFS

The Lenape believed that one all-powerful god, Kishelemukong, ruled over the world. Below him, many lesser spirits served as guardians of the streams, the clouds, the trees, and the harvest. One spirit helped the hunters find game. During certain ceremonies, hunters wore masks depicting the game spirit. One side of the spirit mask was red, and the other black.

Nearly every people on Earth has a story of the creation. In the creation story of the Lenape, Kishelemukong brought a great turtle up from the depths of the world. The turtle grew and grew, until it became the North American continent. Human beings burst forth from a giant tree that sprang from the turtle's back. Kishelemukong also created the four directions. The Lenape called the North, East, and West the Three Grandfathers. South was called Our Grandmother Where It Is Warm.

According to mythology of the Lenape, the Grandparents played a dice game year-round. When the South Grandmother began a winning streak, summer breezes fanned the forests. When the North Grandfather's luck improved, the gales of winter set in. The East and West Grandfathers brought spring and fall.

Life for the Lenape went on with only gradual changes over hundreds of years. When the Lenape sighted a ship with billowed sails gliding along the shore in 1524, they could not have guessed the disaster that lay before them.

MINI-BIO

JAMES LONE BEAR REVEY: RESTORING HIS PEOPLE

James Lone Bear Revey (?–1998) grew up in Neptune, New Jersey. He was a descendant of the last Lenape speaker in the state. He studied the beginnings of Lenape culture and worked to keep traditions alive. Revey founded the New Jersey Indian Commission and wrote about Lenape history and crafts. He shared drumming and dancing techniques with both children and adults. He was also involved with the New Jersey Indian Office in Orange. His lifelong work inspired New Jerseyans of Lenape descent to explore their roots and take pride in their heritage.

? **Want to know more?** Visit www.factsfornow.scholastic.com and enter the keywords **New Jersey**.

When European explorers arrived in 1524 and later, life for the Lenape changed forever.

READ ABOUT

It was off the coast of Sandy Hook that Giovanni da Verrazzano briefly anchored. In later years, the area was settled by Europeans.

1660

Bergen becomes the first European settlement in present-day New Jersey

1664 ▶

James, Duke of York, receives New Jersey as a gift

1702

The Jerseys become a single colony

CHAPTER THREE

EXPLORATION AND SETTLEMENT

★

I MAGINE A MORNING IN 1524. Three Lenape children are gathering nuts in the woods near the shore. Glancing out to sea, they spy a strange floating structure, far bigger than the biggest canoe. Above it hang huge "wings." The children race home with the news. Everyone rushes to the beach to look. The strange canoe sails away. On that day, an Italian sea captain named Giovanni da Verrazzano had anchored briefly off Sandy Hook. But he did not return. The Lenape went on with their lives, undisturbed, for another 85 years.

1750

Only a few hundred Lenape remain in New Jersey

1776 ▶

Washington crosses the Delaware to surprise British and Hessian soldiers at Trenton

1787 ▶

New Jersey ratifies the U.S. Constitution and becomes a state

EXPLORATION AND SETTLEMENT

Henry Hudson explored New Jersey and traded with the local Native Americans while trying to find a passage to the Pacific Ocean through North America.

EARLY EXPLORERS

In 1609, an English captain named Henry Hudson sailed up the river that today bears his name. Hudson's ship, the *Half Moon*, flew the Dutch flag. Based on Hudson's expedition, The Netherlands claimed the land around the Hudson River. The Dutch established a trading post on the southern tip of Manhattan and began trading with the Indians for furs. In 1618, they set up a smaller fur trading station across the Hudson at Bergen. Bergen was the first European settlement in present-day New Jersey. The Dutch established another settlement, Pavonia (present-day Jersey City), in 1630.

European Exploration of New Jersey

The colored arrows on this map show the routes taken by explorers and pioneers between 1524 and 1630.

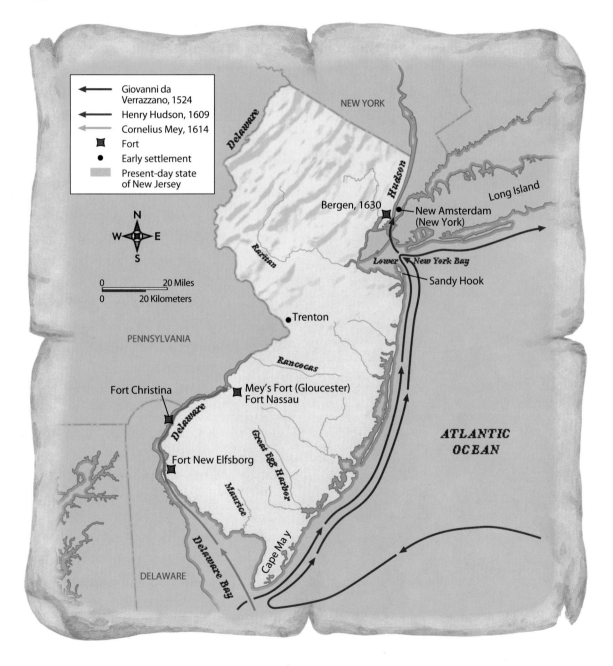

Giovanni da Verrazzano, 1524
Henry Hudson, 1609
Cornelius Mey, 1614
Fort
Early settlement
Present-day state of New Jersey

NEW YORK

Delaware

Hudson

Raritan

Long Island

Bergen, 1630

New Amsterdam (New York)

Lower New York Bay

Sandy Hook

N
W E
S

0   20 Miles
0   20 Kilometers

Trenton

PENNSYLVANIA

Rancocas

Fort Christina

Mey's Fort (Gloucester)
Fort Nassau

Delaware

Great Egg Harbor

ATLANTIC OCEAN

Fort New Elfsborg

Maurice

Cape May

Delaware Bay

DELAWARE

NAMING NEW JERSEY

New Jersey is sprinkled with names from European history. The Hudson River was named after Henry Hudson. Cape May is named for Captain Cornelis Mey (the English spelling was Cornelius May). And Bergen County was named for the Dutch word for "mountains."

Farther south, Dutch captain Cornelis Mey explored Delaware Bay in 1623. In 1638, a Swedish company set up trading posts on the Delaware's New Jersey side. In 1655, Dutch traders drove the Swedes away and took over the Delaware River settlements. The Swedish settlement lasted only 17 years.

The Dutch didn't hold on to their territory for long. In 1664, King Charles II of England studied his maps and gave New Netherland to his beloved brother James, the Duke of York. An English naval fleet arrived at New Netherland and pointed its cannons at the tiny settlement on Manhattan. Not a shot was fired. The Dutch surrendered, and New Netherland became New York. The duke gave the name New Jersey to the land that lay between the Hudson, the Delaware, and the sea.

Almost at once, the Duke of York appointed Richard Nicolls the first royal governor of New York and New Jersey. But a year later, to Nicolls's dismay, the duke handed over New Jersey to two of the king's best friends, Lord John Berkeley and Sir George Carteret. Berkeley and Carteret split New Jersey into two colonies, East Jersey and

Following the passing of his brother, Charles II, James, the Duke of York (right), was crowned King of England on April 23, 1685.

West Jersey. After some years of confusion, the land was surrendered to the British government. And that action united the Jerseys into a single colony in 1702.

THE FATE OF THE LENAPE

At first, the Lenape welcomed the Europeans. The white strangers brought glass beads, iron kettles, wool blankets, guns, and a fiery drink called rum. The Lenape (or Delaware, as the Europeans called them) traded furs for these tempting European goods.

Unknowingly, the Europeans also brought small-pox, measles, tuberculosis, and other diseases. The Indians had not been exposed to these illnesses before, and their bodies had no **immunity** to them. European diseases wiped out entire Lenape villages. When the Europeans arrived, between 10,000 and 20,000 Lenape lived in today's New Jersey. By 1750, only a few hundred remained. Historians believe that European diseases killed 90 percent of the Lenape people.

More and more Europeans poured into New Jersey. They pushed the Lenape off the land where they had lived for hundreds of years. War raged between the Indians and settlers from 1643 to 1645. In the end, the Indians were badly outnumbered. Eventually, European settlers drove most of the Lenape out of New Jersey. Some went to Canada, and others made their way west. Many Lenape wound up settling in Oklahoma, far from the sea where they once fished and gathered oysters.

PLOWING THE LAND

The Dutch had been happy with small trading stations in New Jersey. But the British had bigger ideas.

As a consolation prize for taking New Jersey from Richard Nicolls, the Duke of York gave him a sliver of New Jersey called Staten Island. It later became part of New York City.

WORD TO KNOW

immunity *natural protection against disease*

European settlers built homes and worked on farms, and cities such as Newark were created.

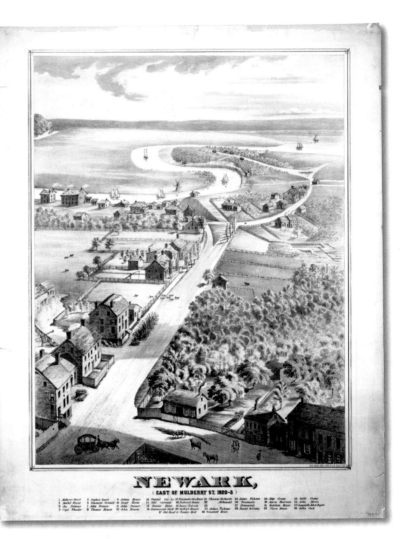

NEWARK,
(EAST OF MULBERRY ST. 1820–5)

HOW DID INDIAN MILLS GET ITS NAME?

Presbyterian minister John Brainerd wanted to start a town where the Lenape could become Christians and support themselves through their work. In 1759, he established Brotherton, an Indian community, in Burlington County. He helped the Lenape open a gristmill to grind wheat into flour. Brotherton went downhill after Brainerd left in 1777, and it closed in 1802. Today, the town of Indian Mills stands on the site of Brotherton, America's first Indian reservation.

They wanted to build a thriving colony. Berkeley and Carteret encouraged people to settle in New Jersey. Many families moved south from New England. The soil in New England was hard to plow because it was full of stones. Central New Jersey offered rich farmland that was almost stone-free.

Berkeley and Carteret allowed New Jerseyans to follow whatever religion they chose. Members of the Society of Friends, or Quakers, were drawn to New Jersey by the promise of religious freedom. The

New Jersey: From Territory to Statehood
(1618–1787)

This map shows the original New Jersey territory and the area (outlined in purple) that became the state of New Jersey in 1787.

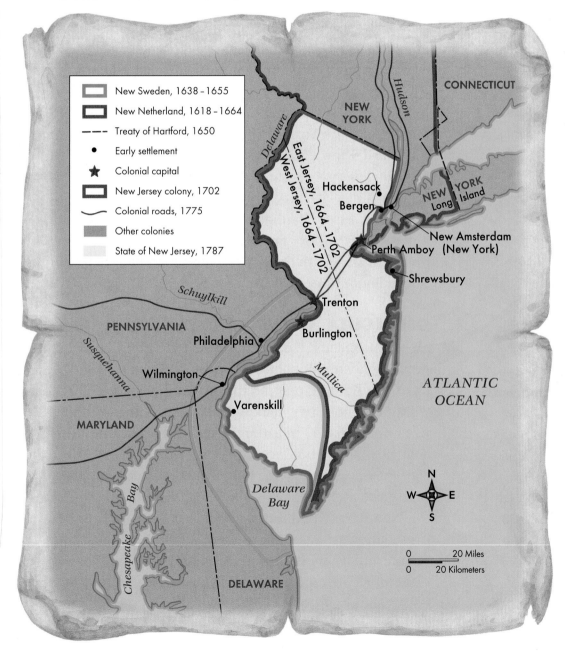

Legend:
- New Sweden, 1638–1655
- New Netherland, 1618–1664
- Treaty of Hartford, 1650
- • Early settlement
- ★ Colonial capital
- New Jersey colony, 1702
- Colonial roads, 1775
- Other colonies
- State of New Jersey, 1787

CONNECTICUT

NEW YORK

Hudson

Delaware

East Jersey, 1664–1702

West Jersey, 1664–1702

Hackensack

Bergen

NEW YORK
Long Island

New Amsterdam (New York)

Perth Amboy

Shrewsbury

Schuylkill

PENNSYLVANIA

Philadelphia

Trenton

Burlington

Mullica

Susquehanna

Wilmington

Varenskill

ATLANTIC OCEAN

MARYLAND

Delaware Bay

Chesapeake Bay

DELAWARE

N
W E
S

0   20 Miles
0   20 Kilometers

Quakers believe that all humans are equal in the eyes of God. They do not think that money or rank makes anyone better than anybody else. They oppose warfare in any form, and they reject all violence. Quakers dress plainly and try to live a simple, quiet lifestyle.

The level fields of central New Jersey produced rich harvests. Cornfields rippled higher than a tall man's head. Hunterdon County produced so much wheat that it became known as "the breadbasket of the colonies." New Jersey farmers raised enough food to feed themselves, and they had plenty more to sell in the cities. New York to the north and Philadelphia to the south were eager for the fruits and vegetables of New Jersey's gardens.

Farming wasn't the only way to earn a living in colonial New Jersey. Tanneries, factories that turn animal hides into leather, opened in Newark. Glassmaking flourished in Salem County. Miners along the Kittatinny Ridge dug into veins of copper and iron ore.

DIFFICULT LIVES

Most Europeans who came to New Jersey and the other English colonies were poor and could afford to cross the Atlantic only as **indentured servants**. They worked without pay, usually for seven years, and their lives were hard—but they eventually became free. Another large number of people, Africans and some Native Americans, were forced into slavery, and they rarely became free.

New Jersey had more slaves than any other northern colony. In 1726, there were about 2,600 enslaved people. In 1745, the number had grown to 4,700. By 1800, one of every eight residents of New Jersey was enslaved, a total of 12,422. Since slaves had no rights

WORD TO KNOW

indentured servants *people who work for others under contract, usually for a specific number of years and for no pay (except food and shelter)*

The first Quaker meetinghouse in Burlington, New Jersey. It was built in 1683, with a hexagonal, or six-sided, design.

under the law, their lives were far worse than those of indentured servants. Many tried to gain their freedom, and some whites, particularly Quakers, helped them escape and form antislavery societies.

Leaders in colonial New Jersey tried to keep people in line by passing harsh laws. For swearing or getting drunk, a person could be whipped in the town square. A thief could be put to death if he was convicted three times. Punishments for African Americans could be far harsher—even barbaric. In 1736, two slaves who set fire to a barn in Hackensack were burned at the stake.

MINI-BIO

JOHN WOOLMAN: THE QUAKER PREACHER

As a storekeeper in Mount Holly, John Woolman (1720–1772) was once asked to write a bill of sale for an African slave. Woolman was horrified. He belonged to the Society of Friends and despised slavery. Woolman became a traveling Quaker preacher. Wherever he went, he spoke against slavery and war. In 1754, he published a pamphlet titled "Some Considerations on the Keeping of Negroes Recommended to the Professors of Christianity of Every Denomination." It is thought to be the first antislavery publication in the colonies. His journal is an important record of his work and Quaker beliefs.

? Want to know more? Visit www.factsfornow .scholastic.com and enter the keywords **New Jersey**.

SEE IT HERE!

THE GLEAMING LIGHT

During the 1700s, many ships were wrecked off the New Jersey shore. In 1764, New Jersey's first lighthouse sent its beams to guide approaching vessels. The Sandy Hook Lighthouse still gleams today. It is the oldest operating lighthouse in the United States.

GROWING UNREST

In 1754, fighting broke out between Britain and France and their Native American allies for control of North America. This was the start of the French and Indian War (1754–1763), which the British eventually won. Although New Jersey was not directly threatened by the conflict, hundreds of the colony's men volunteered to fight for the British.

Sparks flared between Great Britain and its colonies in 1765. In that year, the British Parliament passed a law called the Stamp Act. Colonists needing legal documents, such as a will or a deed, had to buy a government-issued stamp. This was a form of taxation. The colonists were outraged. They had no representatives in Parliament. What right did the British have to pass laws affecting colonists' lives?

Although the king **repealed** the Stamp Act, a series of other taxes followed. Some people muttered about breaking away from England altogether. In New Jersey, opinion was sharply divided. Some New Jerseyans, known as **Tories**, remained loyal to the British. Others argued for freedom from British rule.

On December 22, 1774, a British sea captain unloaded several chests of tea on the dock at Greenwich, New Jersey. At the time, the British government taxed imported tea. The year before, angry

A committee headed by Thomas Jefferson (in the red vest) presents a draft of the Declaration of Independence to John Hancock, the president of the Continental Congress.

Bostonians had protested the tax by dumping a cargo of tea into Boston Harbor. New Jersey was less rebellious than Massachusetts, and the captain didn't expect trouble. He couldn't have been more wrong! A group of Greenwich men disguised themselves as Indians, seized the tea, and burned it. This incident is remembered today as the Greenwich Tea Party. In 1908, citizens erected a monument in the old marketplace in Greenwich to commemorate the burning of the cargo of British tea.

In 1774, each of the colonies sent delegates to a Continental Congress in Philadelphia. This was a first step toward forming a new government. The Second Continental Congress met the following year. On July 4, 1776, delegates from each of the 13 colonies adopted the Declaration of Independence. Great Britain fought to hold on to the colonies. The rebels fought for independence in a war called the American Revolution.

WORDS TO KNOW

repealed *withdrew; undid*

Tories *people who remained loyal to the British during the American Revolution*

On December 25, 1776, General George Washington and a small army of 2,400 men crossed the Delaware River on their way to Trenton, New Jersey.

WORD TO KNOW

infamous *famously terrible*

NEW JERSEY'S PAUL REVERE

On the night of July 1, 1776, a band of New Jersey militiamen kept watch at Sandy Hook. They noticed a fleet of British warships sailing south along the coast. The British were on the move, planning to control the colonists. Militia colonel Nathaniel Scudder galloped all night to carry the news to colonial headquarters at Burlington. Scudder's all-night gallop is sometimes compared to the ride of Massachusetts patriot Paul Revere.

THE CROSSROADS OF THE REVOLUTION

During the Revolution, New Jersey was bitterly divided. About half of all New Jerseyans were Tories. Tories and rebels attacked one another viciously. They looted and burned one another's houses. General George Washington, who was in charge of the Continental army, remarked that "the conduct of the Jerseys is most **infamous**."

Early in the war, the British fortified themselves at Trenton. To strengthen their army, they hired soldiers from the German province of Hesse. These soldiers were known as Hessians. The British had driven Washington's army into Pennsylvania, and they thought they had nothing to worry about through the winter.

The Hessians at Trenton celebrated Christmas 1776 with plenty of food and laughter. At last, they tumbled into their bunks to sleep. In a fleet of rowboats, Washington's army crossed the Delaware and took Trenton by surprise. The Hessians awoke to shouts, stamping feet, and the rattle of musket fire. Washington easily captured the British garrison. A week later, he took Princeton, 15 miles (24 km) away. The victories at Trenton and Princeton boosted the morale of the Continental Army. Washington led his troops north to Morristown, where they camped for the winter.

Picture Yourself . . .

in Washington's Army

It's late at night. You're crowded into a tiny hut with 11 other soldiers. Wind howls outside. It's probably snowing—again! You don't want to peek out and see. All you can think about is food. You remember the last dinner your mother served for you. A freshly killed hen, along with greens from the kitchen garden. That was the night before you joined General Washington to fight the British. Whatever made you think that was a good idea? Tonight at the mess tent, you ate a stale chunk of bread and a bowl of what they called soup—bits of gristle swimming in hot water.

No use thinking about what you can't have. Listening to the wind, you huddle under your blanket and drift off to sleep.

The Continental Army was victorious in the Battle of Trenton.

Q8 WHAT WERE THE MOST IMPORTANT BATTLES FOUGHT IN NEW JERSEY?

A8 The Battle of Trenton, December 26, 1776; the Second Battle of Trenton, January 2, 1777; the Battle of Princeton, January 3, 1777; and the Battle of Monmouth, June 28, 1778.

Washington's army spent another winter at Morristown, arriving in December 1779. It was one of the most brutal winters of the long war. Eighteen separate blizzards buried the men in their tents! Supply wagons with food couldn't get through. Washington wrote that his half-starved men "ate every kind of horse food but hay."

During the American Revolution, New Jersey was the pathway between New York and Philadelphia. While he was commander in chief of the Continental army, Washington spent about one-fourth of his time in New Jersey. He spent more time in New Jersey than in any other state.

The British were defeated at the Battle of Yorktown, Virginia, in 1781. The war finally ended in 1783 with the signing of the Treaty of Paris. The 13 former colonies struggled to knit themselves into an independent nation. At first, they were completely disorganized. They couldn't even decide where to locate their capital! The government met briefly in Trenton, and later in Princeton. Finally, in the summer of 1787, delegates from all of the former colonies, now called states, gathered in Philadelphia. Through the long, hot summer, they hammered out a new set of governing laws, or constitution. New Jerseyans worried that the bigger states, such as New York and Virginia, would have too much control in the new government.

MINI-BIO

SAMUEL SUTPHEN: FREEDOM FIGHTER

Samuel Sutphen (1747–?) was one of many African Americans from New Jersey who fought in the American Revolution. Sutphen served as a foot soldier with the Continental Army for three years. He fought in New Jersey and parts of New York. Although he fought for freedom for the colonies, the war did not help him gain freedom from slavery. After the war, Sutphen was forced to return to his owner in Somerset County. He spent 20 more years in slavery before finally buying his freedom. In 1834, he dictated his memoir to a local doctor, who wrote it down word for word.

 Want to know more? Visit www.factsfornow .scholastic.com and enter the keywords **New Jersey**.

The Battle of Yorktown marked the defeat of the British forces, but the official end of the war would not come until the Treaty of Paris, in 1783.

They argued that each state, big or small, should have the same number of representatives. Their idea was called the New Jersey Plan.

In the end, the U.S. Constitution created a Congress with two houses: the House of Representatives and the Senate. The bigger the state, the more members it would send to the House of Representatives. But the New Jersey Plan was accepted for the Senate. Whether it is large or small, every state elects two senators. New Jersey was satisfied with the plan for Congress. It became the third state to **ratify** the U.S. Constitution.

WORD TO KNOW

ratify *approve*

50

READ ABOUT

The Great Falls of the Passaic River played a significant role in the early industrial development of New Jersey.

1804 ►
Alexander Hamilton dies after a duel at Weehawken

1836
The Morris Canal is completed

1840s
Thousands of Irish immigrants arrive

CHAPTER FOUR

GROWTH AND CHANGE

★

O N JULY 4, 1792, A GROUP OF MEN GATHERED AT THE FOOT OF THE GREAT FALLS OF THE PASSAIC RIVER. Their leader was Alexander Hamilton. Hamilton wanted to build a great industrial city— named Paterson after New Jersey's second governor, William Paterson—with the falls at its heart.

1870
*Thomas Mundy
Peterson casts a vote
in Perth Amboy*

1887 ►
*James Still publishes his
autobiography*

1913
*Paterson workers
go on strike*

FACTORIES AND FARMS

In 1791, Hamilton and a group of investors founded an organization called the Society for Establishing Useful Manufactures (SUM). The New Jersey legislature helped the SUM by not requiring the organization to pay county and township taxes. And it gave the SUM the right to hold property, improve rivers, and build canals. Hamilton asked Pierre Charles L'Enfant, an architect, to plan the town of Paterson and build canals to supply water to the planned manufacturing mills. L'Enfant had big ideas, such as designing many roads that spread out from the center of town. And for the waterpower system, he envisioned a complicated canal system and reservoir.

The SUM eventually dismissed L'Enfant because his ideas were too ambitious. In his place, the group hired Peter Colt. He had a little engineering experience and came up with a simpler plan. As the project continued, Colt constructed a small mill in the planned mill area, because members of the SUM were anxious to begin spinning cotton. The mill was called Bull Mill because an ox supplied the power needed to turn the wheels.

Paterson went on to become a national leader in the textile industry. It earned the nickname the Cotton City. Later, that nickname changed to the Silk City, as factories churned out silk fabrics.

MINI-BIO

ALEXANDER HAMILTON: DREAMER OF INDUSTRY

Born on the Caribbean island of Nevis, Alexander Hamilton (1757–1804) first came to New Jersey when he was 11 years old. Hamilton designed Paterson, the world's first planned industrial city. Years later, he served under President George Washington as the nation's first secretary of the treasury (1789–1795). Hamilton believed that manufacturing would make the country strong. He thought the United States should build a powerful central government that would protect business interests. Hamilton died following a duel with Vice President Aaron Burr in Weehawken.

? **Want to know more?** Visit www.factsfornow .scholastic.com and enter the keywords **New Jersey**.

Glass making was an early industry in Trenton and other New Jersey cities.

If you could travel back to 1830s New Jersey, you would see a patchwork of farms, woods, and meadows. In Paterson, you would see workers bent over weaving machines. In Newark, you would smell the chemicals used in leather tanneries, and you could watch workers making shoes by the thousands. You would see glass-makers at work in Trenton, and you might feel the fierce heat of the fires in the ironworks of Dover and Rockaway. The majority of New Jerseyans were still farmers, but manufacturing was beginning to push farming aside.

GETTING FROM HERE TO THERE

In 1808, a noisy steam-powered vessel, the *Phoenix*, chugged south along the New Jersey shore. Belching smoke, it made its way from Hoboken, New Jersey, to Philadelphia, Pennsylvania. The *Phoenix* was the first steamboat ever to travel on ocean waters. Soon steamboats sailed regularly back and forth across the Hudson and the Delaware rivers. They carried goods and passengers to Newark, Perth Amboy, Camden, and other ports.

The steamboat wasn't the only invention to change life for New Jerseyans. In 1834, passengers in Camden clambered aboard open cars behind a puffing engine. They hung on to their wooden seats as the engine lurched forward along newly laid tracks. The Camden and Amboy Railroad, with service between Camden and South Amboy, was one of the first railroads to operate in the United States.

In 1825, workers began to dig a giant ditch across northern New Jersey. Construction on the Morris Canal, as the ditch was called, took 11 backbreaking years. When it was finally completed in 1836, the canal was 102 miles (164 km) long. Through a series of locks and ramps, the canal climbed 914 feet (229 m) from Phillipsburg to Lake Hopatcong. From there, it descended 760 feet (232 m) to Jersey City.

The Morris Canal formed a link between the Delaware and Hudson rivers. Canal boats carried coal from Pennsylvania to the factories of New York and northern New Jersey. New Jerseyans were on the move!

HEADING FOR CIVIL WAR

The Declaration of Independence states that "all men are created equal." But that equality didn't include African Americans. Some enslaved people were freed after the Revolution. But thousands were still the property of their owners.

In New Jersey, white Quakers and free African Americans led a movement to **abolish** slavery in the state. Many helped slaves escape through a secret system known as the Underground Railroad. **Fugitive**

WOW

Boats on the Morris Canal passed through a greater change in elevation than boats on any other canal in the world.

WORDS TO KNOW

abolish *to put an end to*

fugitive *someone who is trying to escape or is on the run*

slaves were hidden in houses called stations. Courageous men and women, known as conductors, escorted the escaping slaves farther north.

In 1804, an act calling for the gradual ending of slavery came before the New Jersey legislature. Under this act, enslaved people would continue to live as slaves. Their children, however, would be freed when they were older. Girls would be freed at age 21, and boys at 25. When the law passed, it ensured eventual freedom to children born into slavery after July 4, 1804.

After the Revolution, when northern legislatures began to free slaves, New Jersey adopted gradual **emancipation**. By the mid-1800s, most of the workers in the state's factories were paid employees.

Members of the Underground Railroad helped fugitive slaves find their way to freedom.

WORD TO KNOW

emancipation *the act of freeing people from slavery or other control*

MINI-BIO

JAMES STILL: THE PINELANDS DOCTOR

As the child of enslaved parents, James Still (1812–1885) never had the chance to study medicine. However, he had a deep knowledge of herbal cures that had been used for generations. He used his skill as a healer to help the African Americans of the Pinelands. In 1877, he published his autobiography, *Early Recollections and Life of Dr. James Still*. Many of the ideas in Still's book were years ahead of their time. He argued that both black and white children would benefit if they went to school together.

? **Want to know more?** Visit www.factsfornow .scholastic.com and enter the keywords **New Jersey**.

Q: WHAT IS THE FIFTEENTH AMENDMENT?

A: The founding fathers knew that the U.S. Constitution would need to be added to, or amended, from time to time to cover situations they hadn't thought of. The Fifteenth Amendment gave the right to vote to African American men on February 3, 1870. The very next day, a black man named Thomas Mundy Peterson voted in a Perth Amboy election. Peterson was the first African American to vote in the United States.

In the South, however, many farmers depended on slave labor. As the antislavery movement gathered force in the North, the country became more and more deeply divided. At last, the southern states broke away to form their own nation, the Confederate States of America. The Union (the northern states) and the Confederacy plunged into a devastating civil war.

New Jersey stayed in the Union and fought for the Union cause. But New Jerseyans were not all of one mind about the war. Many mistrusted President Abraham Lincoln. A Bergen newspaper even stated, "So long as there is a dollar left in the public treasury, there will be a nest of thieves, swindlers, and contractors lounging around Old Abe." When Lincoln ordered a **military draft** to raise troops, riots broke out in Newark.

At the same time, thousands of New Jerseyans fought bravely. They wanted to save the Union and end slavery. During the Civil War, 218 officers and 6,082 enlisted men from New Jersey lost their lives.

THE NEW AMERICANS

In the 1840s, thousands of immigrants from Ireland flocked to the United States. Many of them found work in New Jersey's factories. The Irish were fleeing a terrible **famine** in their homeland. The United States offered them the chance for a better life.

Immigration to New Jersey swelled in the decades after the Civil War. Between 1870 and 1900, the state's population nearly doubled. More and more factories

For many immigrants entering the United States through New Jersey and New York, the Statue of Liberty stood as a symbol of hope.

WORDS TO KNOW

military draft *requirement that all eligible persons must register for duty in the armed forces*

famine *period of extreme food shortages and hunger*

SEE IT HERE!

OCEAN GROVE

In the summer of 1869, a group of families camped in tents at a quiet spot on the New Jersey shore. Their leader was a Methodist minister named Rev. William B. Osborn. Osborn wanted to found a summer resort town for Methodists. Ocean Grove, Osborn's community, was run according to strict rules. Drinking and card playing were not permitted. Until 1979, you weren't even allowed to drive a car on Sundays!

The centerpiece of the town is the vast Ocean Grove Auditorium. It covers 1 acre (.4 ha) of land and seats 7,000 people. Today, Ocean Grove is a year-round resort that caters to people of all backgrounds. In the summer, some visitors even camp in tents, much as visitors did in the late 19th century.

WORD TO KNOW

strike *an organized refusal to work, usually to protest wages or working conditions*

opened in cities such as Paterson, Newark, Jersey City, and Passaic. Some well-established New Jerseyans grumbled about the "foreigners" pouring into the state. Many seemed to forget that their own ancestors had come to America from across the Atlantic.

Work in the factories was dirty and exhausting. But a lucky worker might save enough to take the family to the shore for a few days in the summer. What could be more wonderful than cool sea breezes, endless beaches, and saltwater taffy? Ordinary working people vacationed in Atlantic City. The rich visited Long Branch. From their luxury homes, they gazed at the sea and listened to the crash of the waves.

For most factory workers, though, even a few days' vacation was out of the question. Wages were so low that workers could barely afford to buy food and pay their rent. In Paterson, Passaic, Newark, and other factory towns, children worked side by side with adults. Factory children had no time to play and no chance to attend school. Some stood at their looms for 12 to 14 hours a day, usually for six days a week.

Paterson factory bosses finally pushed the silk workers too far. In 1913, 23,000 silk workers speaking dozens of languages went on **strike** against low pay. "All nationalities stood side by side," a journalist reported, and speeches were translated "for the benefit of those who could not understand." The high point of the strike came when striking families walked 23 miles (37 km) from Paterson to New York City's Madison Square Garden to present "The Pageant of the Paterson Strike." An audience of more than 15,000 people attended and raised funds for the strike. But after 14 months, strikers ran out of money and returned to work with few gains.

As New Jersey entered the 20th century, it seemed like a land of great opportunity. There were jobs to be had—though the work was hard—and there were growing cities and towns. People from all over the world knew that New Jersey could be a wonderful place to call home.

In Paterson, many young immigrant women worked as seamstresses for local textile factories.

READ ABOUT

As the 20th century began, people from Europe moved to Newark and helped the city grow.

1912

Woodrow Wilson is elected U.S. president

▲1927

The Holland Tunnel opens

1947

The new state constitution outlaws discrimination

CHAPTER FIVE

MORE MODERN TIMES

IN PATERSON, PASSAIC, JERSEY CITY, AND NEWARK ON A DAY IN 1900, you might have overheard women chatting in Italian as they hung clothes on a clothesline, or children shouting in Russian as they played tag. Newcomers from eastern and southern Europe were pouring into the United States, thousands settling in New Jersey. They brought their languages, foods, music, and festivals. The face of New Jersey was changing.

1970 ▸
Kenneth Gibson becomes Newark's first African American mayor

1997
New Jersey Center for the Performing Arts presents its first concert

2012
Hurricane Sandy slams into New Jersey, killing 37 people

The Holland Tunnel opened in 1927, connecting New Jersey to New York City.

On the Holland Tunnel's opening night in 1927, people were allowed to walk through it. Then it was closed to pedestrians forever. Cars have been pouring through the tunnel ever since.

WORD TO KNOW

fraud *cheating and lying*

CLEANING UP POLITICS

In the early 20th century, powerful politicians controlled New Jersey. These "bosses," as they were called, ruled through bribery and **fraud**. They took every available chance to put their friends in office. The bosses worked hand in hand with big business. Under the bosses, factory wages stayed low to put more money in the factory owners' pockets. When workers tried to fight for better conditions, politicians and businessmen discouraged their efforts.

In 1910, Woodrow Wilson, the president of Princeton University, ran for governor of New Jersey. Wilson came from Virginia, so some New Jerseyans saw him as an outsider. But voters rallied when Wilson promised to **reform** state politics. He won the election by a landslide. As governor, he kept his promises. He fought voter fraud and limited the power of big businesses. He passed a workers' compensation law to help workers who were injured on the job.

Governor Wilson attracted national attention. In 1912, he was elected 28th president of the United States. Wilson left the governor's mansion and moved into the White House.

In 1914, two years after Wilson was elected president, World War I erupted in Europe. In 1917, America entered the war, and thousands of New Jersey soldiers set out to fight. New Jersey's factories made ammunition and weapon parts. The state also built ships that were used in the war, which ended in 1918.

In 1920, New York and New Jersey decided to build a tunnel under the Hudson River. An engineer named Clifford Holland was hired to handle the project. Millions of cars would drive through the tunnel between the states. Holland died before the tunnel was finished, and it was named in his honor. It opened on November 12, 1927. The year 1920 also marked the year women were given the right to vote in the United States. Clara Laddey, Alice Paul, and Allison Turnbull Hopkins were a few of the many New Jersey women who worked for the cause.

HARD TIMES AND WARTIME

During the 1930s, the United States endured a terrible economic depression. All over New Jersey, factories shut their doors. Without wages, hardworking men and women couldn't feed their families. Desperate young people took to the road in search of work.

CORRUPTION!

One of Wilson's staunch supporters in 1910 had been Frank Hague. Hague was a police officer from Jersey City. He climbed Jersey City's political ladder and was elected mayor in 1917. Hague promised to reform **corrupt** city politics. But he turned out to be more corrupt than anyone before him! He used every kind of fraud, bribery, and strong-arm tactic to get his way. Pretty soon he controlled not only Jersey City, but most of the state. He earned the nickname Frank "I Am the Law" Hague. He held office as mayor of Jersey City until 1947.

WORDS TO KNOW

reform *to clean up or improve*

corrupt *characterized by immoral and illegal actions*

MINI-BIO

ALICE PAUL: CHAMPION OF EQUALITY

Growing up in Moorestown, Alice Paul (1885–1977) absorbed many ideas from her Quaker parents. She took to heart their belief that men and women are equal and should have equal rights. Alice Paul became a leader in the movement for woman suffrage in the United States. She organized marches and picket lines in Washington, D.C. Several times she was jailed, and once she was kept in solitary confinement for two weeks! A prison doctor said, "She will die if she must, but she won't give up." Women finally gained the right to vote when the Nineteenth Amendment to the Constitution was ratified in 1920.

? Want to know more? Visit www.factsfornow.scholastic.com and enter the keywords **New Jersey**.

WOW

The George Washington Bridge contains 43,000 tons of steel. Its four main suspension cables are made up of 26,474 twisted wires *each!*

New Jerseyans enjoyed a moment of triumph when the George Washington Bridge opened in 1931. The GW Bridge, as New Jerseyans call it, arches 212 feet (65 m) above the Hudson River. It is the only 14-lane suspension bridge in the world! The bridge has two decks with 8 lanes on the upper deck and 6 on the lower deck.

On December 7, 1941, the nation learned that Japanese planes had bombed the U.S. naval fleet at Pearl Harbor in Hawaii. The United States plunged into another world war, fighting Japan and Germany. Suddenly, New Jersey's factories sprang to life again. Women and men worked around the clock. Mills in Paterson and Passaic turned out uniforms and parachutes. Battleships steamed from the shipyards at Kearny and Hoboken. Thousands of African Americans moved to New Jersey from the South to take jobs in New Jersey's wartime industries.

African Americans came to New Jersey hoping to find better opportunities. Sadly, many met disappointment. In many towns and cities, especially in southern New Jersey, white communities forced black children to attend all-black schools. Most hospitals refused to hire black doctors or nurses. On hot summer days, "whites only" swimming pools banned black families.

African American organizations such as the Urban League and the National Association for the Advancement of Colored People (NAACP) worked to break down such barriers. When the state drafted a new constitution in 1947, lawmakers added a provision against **discrimination**. The 1947 constitution forbade discrimination toward any person in the public schools or the state militia based on religion, race, color, or ancestry. New Jersey was the first state to forbid **segregation** in its public schools.

WORDS TO KNOW

discrimination *unequal treatment based on race, gender, religion, or other factor*

segregation *separation based on race, gender, religion, or other factor*

The civil rights movement in New Jersey was strong in the 1960s. Here, in August 1964, activists and protestors rally in Atlantic City, the site of the Democratic National Convention.

MINI-BIO

PAUL ROBESON: A MAN AHEAD OF HIS TIME

Paul Robeson (1898–1976) was born in Princeton to a father who had escaped from slavery. After graduating from Rutgers University, where he excelled in sports, Robeson went on to earn a law degree at Columbia University. In the 1930s, he mastered a dozen languages and became famous as a Shakespearean actor, movie star, and concert singer. Robeson devoted his life to working for people of all races and fighting unfair government practices. He may have been the most admired American in the world; some people even said he should have been president.

❓ **Want to know more?** Visit www.factsfornow.scholastic.com and enter the keywords **New Jersey**.

The Great Swamp is a natural area that was saved from destruction during the 1950s.

Q8 WHAT IS NEW JERSEY'S MAIN HIGHWAY?

A8 With up to 14 lanes of traffic, the New Jersey Turnpike is the broadest highway in the state.

SUBURBAN LIFE

After World War II ended in 1945, New Jersey enjoyed years of peace and prosperity. Developers cleared woodlands and built houses in blossoming suburbs. Families who could afford to do so began leaving the cities. They bought new homes surrounded by lawns and gardens. The children of immigrants studied to become teachers, lawyers, and doctors.

During the 1950s, plans were afoot for a new airport south of Morristown. The project would have destroyed the Great Swamp, one of New Jersey's most extensive wetlands. Nature lovers rallied to protect the swamp, which is home to hundreds of kinds of birds and animals. The wetlands was saved with the creation of the Great Swamp National Wildlife Refuge in 1960. The refuge preserves 7,600 acres (3,080 ha) of wetlands in Harding Township.

LIVING IN THE CITY

When middle-class families moved from cities to sub-urbs, businesses followed. In the cities, job opportunities shrank, and mayors collected less tax money. Neighborhoods and schools became run-down, while poor whites, Puerto Ricans, and African Americans lived in crowded, dirty, and dangerous areas. Corrupt politicians in Newark and some other cities did little to help these citizens, who worked at low-paying jobs, if they could find work at all. People had little power in their governments.

In July 1967, anger over worsening conditions boiled over in a Newark riot. Mostly young, unemployed, and poor people of color rioted for six days. By the time the National Guard restored order, there were 26 deaths, 1,200 arrests, and a property loss totaling $10 million. The National Guard also ended a smaller riot in Plainfield. A Governor's Commission investigation found the lawmen and the National Guard used "excessive and unjustified force."

The riots did awaken many people to the problems urban families faced and the impact of racial discrimination. Government programs were started to help people in disadvantaged urban areas gain political power. In 1970, Newark elected its first African American mayor, Kenneth Gibson. He worked to increase jobs, improve schools, and build better race relations.

MINI-BIO

KENNETH GIBSON: LEADER OF REFORM

Kenneth Gibson (1932–) was the first African American to become mayor of a northeastern city. He worked to improve housing, health, and education. He tried to open greater job opportunities for African Americans. Gibson's efforts helped to make Newark more attractive to businesses, and several companies opened branches in the city during his years in office. Gibson was elected to four terms as mayor and served until 1986.

? **Want to know more?** Visit www. factsfornow.scholastic.com and enter the keywords **New Jersey**.

Along the boardwalk in Atlantic City. In the 1970s, the city opened casinos and hotels to strengthen the economy.

GAMES, GAMES, GAMES!

Atlantic City's old hotels had grown shabby. The boardwalk needed repair. But everything changed after New Jersey voted to bring gambling casinos to Atlantic City in 1976. Almost overnight, the city became the most popular tourist destination in the United States. Along the boardwalk, a string of luxury hotels welcomed visitors. They offered fine dining, glamorous shows with top performers, and the thrill of games of chance.

The vast Meadowlands Sports Complex also opened in 1976. Once a wasteland of garbage from homes and factories, the Hackensack Meadowlands had been an embarrassment to New Jerseyans. The Meadowlands was transformed with a football stadium and an arena for hockey and basketball games. The sports complex gave residents a sense of pride. Teams that once played in the Meadowlands included the New York Giants and New York Jets (football), the New York Red Bulls (soccer), and the New Jersey Nets (basketball). The sports complex also includes a horse racetrack.

BUILDING FROM THE ASHES

Hoping to raise Newark from the ruins of the 1967 riot, the state government made rebuilding the city a top priority. In 1997, the magnificent New Jersey Center for the Performing Arts presented its first concert. The center reaches out to city dwellers with affordable programs and activities.

In 2007, the Prudential Center was completed. It is the home of the New Jersey Devils (hockey) and Seton Hall's men's basketball team. Each year, dozens of concerts, political rallies, and other sporting events are also staged there.

A bright new addition to the New Jersey landscape is MetLife Stadium, located in the Meadowland Sports Complex. The stadium opened in 2010 as home to football's New York Giants and New York Jets. MetLife replaced Giants Stadium, which was torn down. At a cost of $1.6 billion, MetLife is the most expensive sports stadium ever built.

On September 11, 2001, terrorists attacked the World Trade Center in Lower Manhattan. Many New Jerseyans visited and worked in those towers, which were both destroyed. Approximately 700 New Jersey residents were killed that day. It was a challenge for New Jersey to recover from that tragedy. But the state has proven its ability to survive disaster and build anew.

SEE IT HERE!

THE ELEPHANT ON THE SHORE

Can you picture a building in the shape of a giant elephant? In 1882, a businessman named Robert Lafferty thought a huge elephant on the shore at Margate would be a great tourist attraction. And he was right. The elephant he built, known as Lucy, towers six stories high and weighs 90 tons. Lucy is 38 feet (12 m) long from head to tail. She was built with more than 1,000,000 pieces of wood and 200 kegs of nails.

After Lafferty died, Lucy started falling apart. In 1970, she got a complete makeover. She even became a National Historic Landmark. Now visitors again climb the stairs in her leg, peer through her glass eyes, and enjoy the ocean view from her back.

READ ABOUT

Crowds gather for
the annual Fourth
of July celebration
in Atlantic City in
2012.

CHAPTER SIX

PEOPLE

★

WHEN IT COMES TO PEOPLE, NEW JERSEY HAS PLENTY OF THEM. According to the 2010 census, there are 8,791,894 New Jerseyans. New Jersey is one of the smallest states in area, so where does it put so many people? Not too surprisingly, the vast majority of New Jerseyans are urban dwellers. In all, 95 percent live in cities and towns. Only 5 percent live in rural areas. The Garden State is the most densely populated state in the country!

Rabbi Akiba Lubow displays a Torah scroll to a New Jersey interfaith student group. This was part of an effort to explore different religions and promote respect.

Wyoming, the ninth largest state in size, has only **563,626** people; tiny **New Jersey** is home to **8,791,894 people.**

LIVING IN NEW JERSEY

The state is home to people from a variety of nationalities and backgrounds. In fact, by percentage, New Jersey has the fourth-highest number of Jewish residents in the country and the fourth-highest number of Asian residents. New Jerseyans also speak a wide range of languages, including Spanish, Portuguese, and Italian.

New Jersey is one of the wealthiest states in the nation. However, some big cities still have areas of extreme poverty.

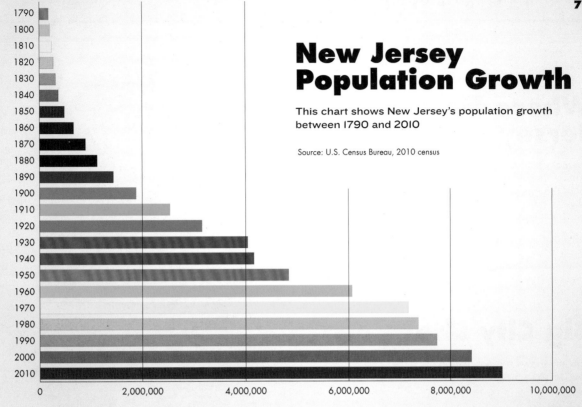

New Jersey Population Growth

This chart shows New Jersey's population growth between 1790 and 2010

Source: U.S. Census Bureau, 2010 census

People QuickFacts

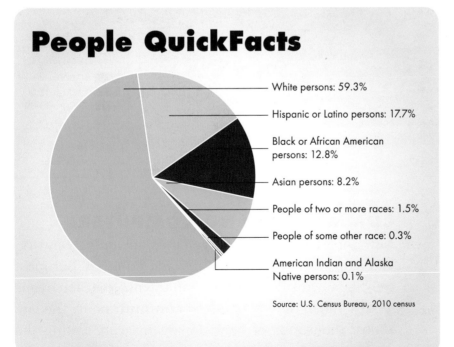

White persons: 59.3%

Hispanic or Latino persons: 17.7%

Black or African American persons: 12.8%

Asian persons: 8.2%

People of two or more races: 1.5%

People of some other race: 0.3%

American Indian and Alaska Native persons: 0.1%

Source: U.S. Census Bureau, 2010 census

Where New Jerseyans Live

The colors on this map indicate population density throughout the state. The darker the color, the more people live there.

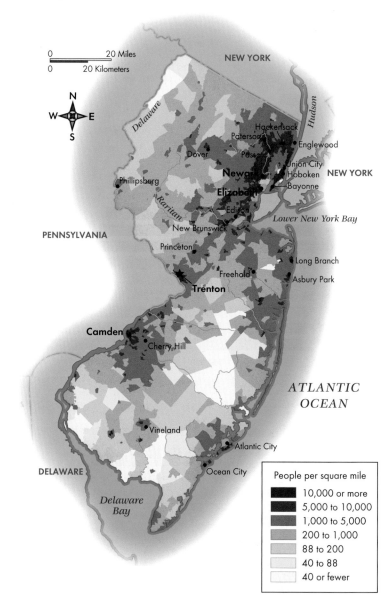

Big City Life

This list shows the population of New Jersey's biggest cities.

Newark	277,140
Jersey City	247,597
Paterson	146,199
Elizabeth	124,969
Trenton	84,913

Source: U.S. Census Bureau, 2010 census

People per square mile

- 10,000 or more
- 5,000 to 10,000
- 1,000 to 5,000
- 200 to 1,000
- 88 to 200
- 40 to 88
- 40 or fewer

WORD TO KNOW

commuters *people who travel to and from work, often from suburbs to cities*

COMMUTERS AND COMPUTERS

New Jersey has several large cities, including Newark, Paterson, Trenton, Jersey City, and Camden. But most New Jerseyans live in suburban towns. New Jerseyans were some of the nation's first **commuters**. By the late 1800s, thousands of New Jerseyans were taking the

ferry every day to work in New York or Philadelphia. When bridges and tunnels were built, commuting got even easier. Many New Jersey towns are nicknamed "bedroom communities." People work in Philadelphia or Manhattan and sleep at home in New Jersey. (People in northern New Jersey often refer to New York as The City, as if it's the only city.)

By the 1990s, more and more people in New Jersey were moving farther from the big cities. They settled in towns that had been forest or farmland only a few years before. Their trips to work got longer and longer. Computers help some New Jerseyans avoid long drives every day. They work at home and communicate with the office by phone and e-mail. There is a name for people who work this way. They are called telecommuters.

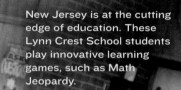

New Jersey is at the cutting edge of education. These Lynn Crest School students play innovative learning games, such as Math Jeopardy.

Per square mile, New Jersey is home to more scientists and engineers than any other place in the world.

IN THE CLASSROOM

Are you looking for a good school? New Jersey is the place to go. This state is considered to have one of the best public school systems in the nation. Some inner-city schools still have some problems, but the state is finding ways to improve education for all New

Jerseyans. In fact, some 54 percent of high school graduates go on to college or university. For this statistic, New Jersey is tied (with Massachusetts) for second in the country. Only North Dakota has a better record (at 59 percent). New Jersey is ranked first in the nation for funding education in K–12 public schools.

The first publicly funded schools in New Jersey opened in 1817. Students had to pay various fees in order to attend. Some New Jerseyans thought public education should be free. Others grumbled about opening "free schools for paupers." Finally, in 1871, the state got rid of fees and started a system of free public schools. Today, all New Jersey children between the ages of 6 and 16 are required to attend school.

New Jersey is home to two of the oldest universities in the United States. Princeton University was founded as the College of New Jersey in 1746. In 1766, Rutgers University, then called Queens College, held its first classes. The two schools have been friendly rivals for more than 200 years. In 1869, Rutgers University and Princeton University did something historic! They played each other in what became the first intercollegiate football game in U.S. history. Who won? Rutgers by a score of 6–4. Today, New Jersey has 14 public and 30 private colleges and universities.

MINI-BIO

ALBERT EINSTEIN: IT'S ALL RELATIVE!

Most people think of Albert Einstein (1879–1955) as the greatest scientist of modern times. Einstein was born in Germany and came to the United States in 1933. He lived in Princeton and did research through Princeton University's Institute for Advanced Studies. Einstein is best known for his Theory of Relativity, which helps explain the beginnings of the universe. His research was key in launching the world into the Atomic Age.

? **Want to know more?** Visit www.factsfornow.scholastic.com and enter the keywords **New Jersey**.

HOW TO TALK LIKE A NEW JERSEYAN

People from northern New Jersey sound a bit like New Yorkers. People from southern Jersey have the hint of a southern lilt. A few words and phrases are unique to parts of New Jersey.

- In South Jersey, a baby carriage is sometimes called a baby coach.
- When New Jerseyans feel chilly, they get goose pimples.
- When talking to more than one person at once, many people in North Jersey say "yous" instead of "you" or "you all."
- A long sandwich filled with lettuce and meat can be called a hoagie.
- When New Jerseyans head for the beach, they say they're going "down the shore."

HOW TO EAT LIKE A NEW JERSEYAN

New Jersey is known as the Garden State—and for good reason! It produces a wide variety of fruits and vegetables, including apples and asparagus, peaches and peppers, cauliflower and cabbage, cranberries and blueberries. But that's not all. It also boasts a great catch of seafood. A delicious treat is a bucket of steamers, or steamed clams, dipped in melted butter. Or try fresh smelts, rolled in cornmeal and deep-fried to a crisp. See the opposite page for some other great New Jersey dishes.

A bucket of steamers is a great summer treat!

Blueberries are sweet tasting and good for you!

MENU

WHAT'S ON THE MENU IN NEW JERSEY?

★ ★ ★

Corn

It comes straight from local farms. What's summer without steaming corn on the cob?

Beefsteak Tomatoes

Another summer favorite. These large round, juicy tomatoes are perfect for topping hamburgers and salads—or great by themselves.

Seafood

New Jerseyans enjoy a variety of ocean fish, including bluefish, porgies, and striped bass. And what is a cherrystone? It's a raw clam served cold and slippery on the half shell. Cherrystones are not for everyone. But people who like them like them a lot.

Saltwater Taffy

Who invented it? Nobody knows for sure. By the 1880s, taffy was sold at fairs in the Midwest. Some shops also sold it at the Jersey shore. According to one story, the name saltwater taffy came from an Atlantic City shopkeeper named David Bradley. One day in 1883, Bradley was mopping up after his store and all his candy had been flooded with seawater. A girl asked to buy some candy, and he said, "Have some of my saltwater taffy!" Since the 1890s, a box of saltwater taffy has been the perfect souvenir after a day at the beach.

TRY THIS RECIPE
Blueberry Cobbler

New Jersey farms produce delicious blueberries. In fact, the blueberry is the state fruit. You can put them on your breakfast cereal, eat them by the handful, or enjoy them in a cobbler. Try this recipe (just be sure to have an adult nearby to help).

Ingredients:
3 tablespoons unsalted butter, melted
2 cups blueberries
1 cup flour
2 teaspoons baking powder
1 cup plus 2 teaspoons sugar
1 teaspoon salt
1 cup milk

Directions:
1. Preheat the oven to 350°.
2. Spread the melted butter over the bottom of a 9-inch glass pie plate. Cover the butter with the blueberries.
3. In a medium-size bowl, mix the flour, baking powder, 1 cup of the sugar, and the salt. Add the milk. When blended, pour the batter over the blueberries. Sprinkle the remaining 2 teaspoons sugar over the batter.
4. Bake 45 to 50 minutes, or until the top is nicely browned.
   Note: This cobbler goes very well with vanilla ice cream.

Blueberry cobbler

A glassblowing team works on a large glass bottle at Wheaton Village in Millville. Glassmaking is a very popular industry in New Jersey.

SEE IT HERE!

THE JERSEY HOMESTEADS MURAL

During the Great Depression in the 1930s, the U.S. government moved a group of unemployed garment workers to rural New Jersey. The group began a farming community called Jersey Homesteads. Ben Shahn (1898–1969) painted the history of Jersey Homesteads in a mural on the wall of the town's elementary school. The town of Jersey Homesteads is now called Roosevelt. You can still see Shahn's mural on the school's wall.

ART AND ARTISTS

Arts and crafts are very much alive in New Jersey today. Fine crafts go back to colonial times. The European colonists discovered rich deposits of quartz in southern New Jersey. They used quartz sand to make beautiful glassware. Two German families, the Wistars and the Stangers, ran important glassmaking businesses. Today, collectors prize their beautifully tinted bowls and bottles. The colonists also began to make pottery with clay they found along New Jersey's streams and rivers. By the early 1800s, New Jersey potters were flourishing, especially in and around Flemington. A type of pottery from this period, called Jersey stoneware, is very valuable today.

Other crafts also date back to colonial times. Dutch patterns can be seen in early hand-stitched quilts. Ironworkers in Sussex and Warren counties made ornate gates and railings.

The first American sculptor to earn fame was a woman from Bordentown named Patience Lovell Wright. She became known for her wax statues of famous people of her time. She lived in London during the American Revolution, and she was a spy for the American side.

Until the 1930s, most New Jersey artists left the state to display their work. Then the Newark Museum started to encourage local painters and sculptors by putting their work on exhibit. Other museums followed. Today, New Jersey offers artists many opportunities to share their work with the public.

In the 1980s, New Jersey saw a rich crafts revival. The state sponsored a monthlong celebration of crafts in 1985. The festival was called All Join Hands. Seventy crafts fairs, workshops, and exhibits were held throughout the state. Potters, quilters, woodworkers, weavers, and other craftspeople took part.

NEW JERSEY WRITERS

New Jersey has been home to many classic writers. Poet Walt Whitman (1819–1892) celebrated democracy and city life in his work. In 1873, Whitman moved to Camden, where he lived until his death. He wrote some of his best-known poems in Camden, such as "When Lilacs Last in the Dooryard Bloom'd" and "Captain, My Captain" in honor of Abraham Lincoln.

Stephen Crane (1871–1900) was born in Newark. His novel *The Red Badge of Courage* tells the story of

MINI-BIO

WENDELL BROOKS: PICTURING THE BLUES

Printmaker Wendell Brooks (1939–) was born in Alabama, where he absorbed the music of the African Americans of the Deep South. In 1971, he settled in Ewing, New Jersey, to teach art at The College of New Jersey. He has won international recognition for his prints. His work encourages viewers to find strength and joy, even in times of suffering. Brooks draws inspiration from many sources, from southern blues music to Buddhist meditation.

? Want to know more? Visit www.factsfornow .scholastic.com and enter the keywords **New Jersey**.

WOW

The poem that begins, "I think that I shall never see /A poem lovely as a tree," was written in 1913 by Joyce Kilmer (1886–1918) of New Brunswick.

Anne Morrow Lindbergh, of Englewood, with her husband, Charles Lindbergh, advanced the field of American aviation. She was also a respected writer.

WILLIAM CARLOS WILLIAMS: THE DOCTOR POET

For 40 years, William Carlos Williams (1883–1963), the son of an English father and a Puerto Rican mother, took care of sick children in Rutherford. When he wasn't treating measles, he wrote poetry. Williams said that his work as a doctor helped him understand how people felt and thought, and that made him a better poet. His long poem "Paterson" tells the story of the city on the Great Falls of the Passaic River. Williams won the Pulitzer Prize in 1963.

? Want to know more? Visit www.factsfornow .scholastic.com and enter the keywords **New Jersey**.

a Civil War soldier. Amazingly, Crane wrote vividly about war even though he never experienced a battle himself. Here is an example from the book: "Another [soldier] had the gray seal of death already upon his face. His lips were curled in hard lines and his teeth were clinched. His hands were bloody from where he had pressed them upon his wound. He seemed to be awaiting the moment when he should pitch headlong. He stalked like the specter of a soldier, his eyes burning with the power of a stare into the unknown."

Anne Morrow Lindbergh (1906–2001) was born in Englewood and is remembered for *Gifts from the Sea*, a collection of observations about her life, work, and relationship with her family. She also published some of her diaries. An accomplished pilot, she was married to Charles Lindbergh. They lived for a number of years in Hopewell.

ON STAGE AND SCREEN

The Garden State has produced an amazing array of performers. Grammy Award–winning singer Bruce Springsteen was born in Long Branch and grew up in Freehold Borough. He often sings about his home state in his

JUDY BLUME: WRITER FOR KIDS

Judy Blume (1938–) grew up in Elizabeth. As a child, she loved to make up stories, but she never imagined that she could become a writer. When she had children of her own, she began to write her stories down on paper. Her books quickly became popular with kids all over the world. In books such as Superfudge and Blubber, she captured the feelings of ordinary kids dealing with the problems and joys of growing up. Though she has lived in many parts of the country, New Jersey is the setting for most of Blume's novels.

Want to know more? Visit www.factsfornow .scholastic.com and enter the keywords **New Jersey**.

New Jersey musician Bruce Springsteen and wife Patti Scialfa in Asbury Park. They are both members of the E Street Band.

MINI-BIO

QUEEN LATIFAH: LADIES FIRST

Until the arrival of Queen Latifah (1970–), male performers ruled the rap music scene. Queen Latifah changed that forever. Her music reflected her spirit—the spirit of a strong, fearless woman who wouldn't let anyone take her down. She was born Dana Owens in Newark, and she later moved to Irvington and Wayne. Queen Latifah became an instant star with her album *All Hail the Queen*. Queen Latifah has hosted a TV talk show and appeared in several movies. She usually plays the role of a woman who knows how to stand up for herself.

? Want to know more? Visit www.factsfornow .scholastic.com and enter the keywords **New Jersey**.

songs. In fact, his debut album in 1973 was titled *Greetings from Asbury Park, N.J.* Decades later, he is proud of his Jersey roots and volunteers to help revitalize areas such as Asbury Park. Actor and recording artist Lauryn Hill grew up in South Orange. She was a member of the Grammy Award-winning group the Fugees with fellow New Jerseyans Wyclef Jean and Pras Michel.

Critically acclaimed actors such as Kevin Spacey, Meryl Streep, Danny DeVito, and Jack Nicholson are all from New Jersey. And Emmy Award–winning comedian Jon Stewart hails from Lawrence Township.

Are you a Spider-Man fan? Kirsten Dunst (who played girlfriend Mary Jane in the first 3 movies) is from Point Pleasant.

What may have been the first baseball game was played in Hoboken on June 19, 1846. The game was played between two teams from New York, the Knickerbockers and the Nines.

GARDEN STATE SPORTS

Well, their team names may say they are from New York, but both the Giants and the Jets are professional teams that play at MetLife stadium at the Meadowlands Sports Complex in East Rutherford. The Giants have been Super Bowl champs four times, in 1986, 1990, 2007, and 2011. The Jets won the 1968 title.

The New Jersey Devils play hockey at the Prudential Center in Newark. The team has captured the Stanley Cup three times, 1995, 2000, and 2003.

Lots of great athletes have ties to New Jersey. Bill Bradley was born in Missouri, but he was an All-American basketball player for Princeton University. He went on to play professionally for the New York Knicks. He later entered politics and served as New Jersey's U.S. senator. Larry Doby grew up in Paterson and played baseball for the Newark Eagles in the Negro Leagues. He joined the Cleveland Indians in 1947, becoming just the second African American to play in the major leagues. Tennis player Althea Gibson was born in South Carolina and raised in New York. But after winning Wimbledon and other championships, she became the New Jersey state commissioner of athletics and made her home in East Orange.

Athletes and artists, movie stars and musicians, teachers and scientists—so many different people make New Jersey their home. And it's easy to see why! The state is a great place to work, live, and play.

Giants Stadium, at the Meadowlands, is the only football field in the National Football League that is home to two teams: the New York Giants and the New York Jets.

READ ABOUT

Governor Chris Christie speaks before a joint session of the New Jersey congress.

CHAPTER SEVEN

GOVERNMENT

★

IN DOWNTOWN TRENTON, YOU CAN'T MISS THE GOLDEN DOME OF THE NEW JERSEY STATE CAPITOL. It rises above all the other buildings around it. The state capitol is the building where much of the business of government takes place. What goes on inside? State representatives make laws that help New Jersey run better. Some laws deal with health and medicine. Some provide funding for public schools and educational programs. Other laws protect animals and parks.

Capitol Facts

Here are some fascinating facts about New Jersey's state capitol.

- Exterior height: 145 feet (44 m)
- Interior height: 105 feet (32 m)
- Amount of cast iron used in the dome: 100 tons
- Number of pieces of cast iron used in the dome: 667
- Number of stories in the capitol: 3

The New Jersey capitol is covered with very thin gold leaf. In all, the gold on the capitol dome weighs only 1 pound (0.5 kilogram).

A motto inscribed on the capitol dome reads *Fiat Justitia Ruat Coelum*. That's Latin for "There must be Justice even though the Heavens Fall."

WHERE IT ALL HAPPENS

Philadelphia architect Jonathan Doane designed the original statehouse, which was built in 1792. Over the next 200 years, lawmakers changed and expanded the building to suit their needs. A dome was added, and more offices were built. In 1885, the building suffered a terrible fire, but the structure was rebuilt. Today, it is the second-oldest state capitol in continuous use.

MAKING THE RULES

The first state constitution was passed on July 2, 1776. This was two days before the Second Continental Congress declared independence from Britain. New Jersey was represented by Richard Stockton, John Witherspoon, Francis Hopkinson, John Hart, and

Capital City

This map shows places of interest in Trenton, New Jersey's capital city.

Abraham Clark. They were among the men who signed the Declaration of Independence.

New Jersey's government is based on its current constitution. New Jersey's current state constitution was approved, or ratified, in 1947. Like the government of the United States, New Jersey's government is divided into three branches: the executive branch, the legislative branch, and the judicial branch.

MINI-BIO

KIM GUADAGNO: CRIME-FIGHTING POLITICIAN

Kim Guadagno (1959–) was elected the first lieutenant governor of New Jersey in 2009 as the running mate of Governor Chris Christie. She also serves as the secretary of state of New Jersey. Born in Waterloo, Iowa, Guadagno studied law and served in the New Jersey criminal court system. In 2007, she was elected the sheriff of Monmouth County, where she fought crime and started several successful antidrug and anti-gang programs.

? **Want to know more?** Visit www.factsfornow.scholastic.com and enter the keywords **New Jersey**.

New Jersey State Government

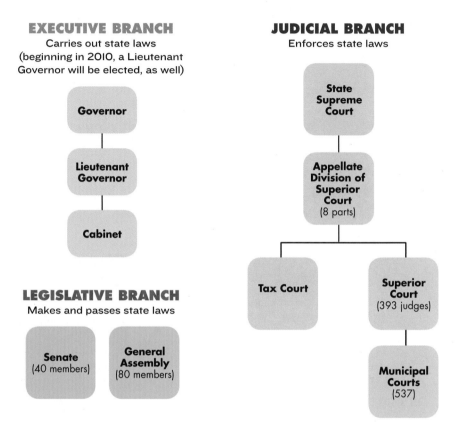

EXECUTIVE BRANCH

Carries out state laws
(beginning in 2010, a Lieutenant
Governor will be elected, as well)

- Governor
- Lieutenant Governor
- Cabinet

JUDICIAL BRANCH

Enforces state laws

- State Supreme Court
- Appellate Division of Superior Court (8 parts)
  - Tax Court
  - Superior Court (393 judges)
    - Municipal Courts (537)

LEGISLATIVE BRANCH

Makes and passes state laws

- Senate (40 members)
- General Assembly (80 members)

Representing New Jersey

This list shows the number of elected officials who represent New Jersey, both on the state and national levels.

OFFICE	NUMBER	LENGTH OF TERM
State senators	40	4 years
General assembly members	80	2 years
U.S. senators	2	6 years
U.S. representatives	12	2 years
Presidential electors	14	—

THE EXECUTIVE BRANCH

The governor is the head of the executive branch. He or she oversees the state budget and works with lawmakers to create programs that serve the state. The governor appoints leaders of various government committees. The first New Jersey election to include voting for a lieutenant governor was held in 2009. Previously, that position did not exist in the state government.

THE LEGISLATIVE BRANCH

New Jersey's state legislature has two sections, or houses. The lower house is called the assembly, and the upper house is called the senate. Representatives from throughout the state create bills that become laws. They work to keep the interests of New Jerseyans in mind and make the state a safe and fair place to live.

THE JUDICIAL BRANCH

New Jersey's court system is a little like a pyramid. At the base are the municipal courts in most towns. Each county has a county court. Cases can be appealed through a system of superior courts all the way to the state supreme court in Trenton. The supreme court is at the top of the pyramid.

CHALLENGES FOR THE STATE

Many companies in New Jersey are guilty of dumping dangerous materials into the state's waters and wild areas. One spot is in Ringwood, where an automobile manufacturing company is accused of dumping waste. This area was made a Superfund cleanup site, but the automaker did not fulfill its obligations to clean it up. A Native American group had been complaining about this site for some time. And it eventually sued the automaker for polluting their environment. In the end, workers removed 20,000 tons of **toxic waste** from the site.

Other issues facing New Jersey include high property taxes and high automobile insurance premiums. State leaders are trying a number of measures to make New Jersey a more affordable place to live.

SEE IT HERE!

DRUMTHWACKET

The governor of New Jersey lives in a mansion in Princeton. It has the unusual name of Drumthwacket. The name comes from Scottish Gaelic words meaning "wooded hill." Parts of the building date back to 1845. Drumthwacket has been the governor's official home since 1981. The grounds include gardens, greenhouses, and even a small dairy farm. Six rooms in the mansion are open to visitors.

WORD TO KNOW

toxic waste *leftover material from factories that can be poisonous*

NEW JERSEY PRESIDENTS

Grover Cleveland (1837–1908) was the only U.S. president to be elected to two nonconsecutive terms. He was elected as the 22nd president in 1884 and as the 24th in 1892. Cleveland was born in Caldwell and is the only native New Jerseyan ever to become president.

Thomas Woodrow Wilson (1856–1924) was born in Virginia. He served as president of Princeton University from 1902 to 1910, when he became governor of New Jersey. In 1912, he was elected as the 28th president of the United States. After World War I, Wilson tried unsuccessfully to have the United States join the League of Nations, a forerunner of the United Nations.

Think About It: Land in Danger

THINK ABOUT IT!

In 2013, a group of Lenape and Cherokee Indians filed suit against a company that plans to build a gas pipeline in New Jersey and Pennsylvania. The group claims the pipeline will destroy tribal lands and sacred burial grounds. "There are a significant number of ancient sacred artifacts and remains of petitioner's [the group that filed the suit] ancestors resting throughout the targeted areas," the group said. The group also says that the pipeline violates both their agreements with the federal government and an 18th-century local treaty. The lawsuit may take years to settle.

LOCAL GOVERNMENT

New Jersey has 565 cities and towns. The state is divided into 21 counties. Each of those cities, towns, and counties has its own local government. Trials take place at county courthouses. And cities and towns elect their own mayors and school boards.

The government of New Jersey is guided by the will of the state's people. New Jerseyans suggest new laws or ask for the repeal of old ones. New Jersey schoolchildren have had a direct impact in the selection of some of the state's symbols. The efforts of middle-school children from Lake Hopatcong helped the brook trout to become the state fish. In 2003, children from Brick launched a successful campaign for the blueberry to become the state fruit. For issues big and small, New Jerseyans have a say in how their state is run.

New Jersey Counties

This map shows the 21 counties in New Jersey. Trenton, the state capital, is indicated with a star.

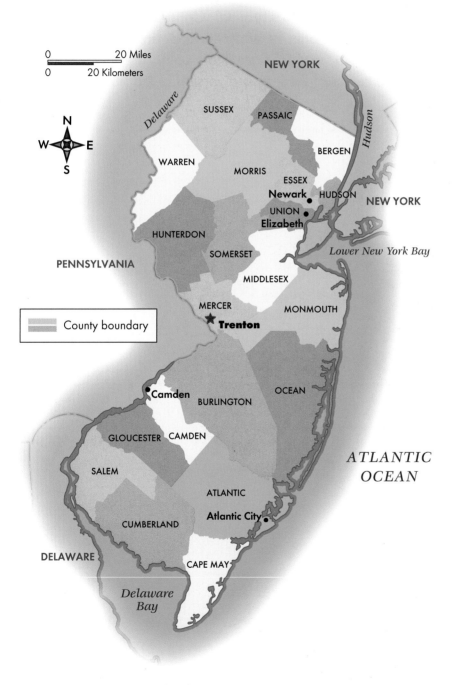

State Flag

New Jersey's state flag was adopted in 1896. It features the state colors of Jersey blue and buff (for the background). General George Washington chose these colors in 1779, after he was headquartered in the state during the Revolutionary War. These were the military colors used by the New Jersey troops. In the center of the flag is a version of the state seal.

State Seal

The state seal was designed in 1777. Several state symbols are included in the seal. The horse head stands for speed and strength. The horse is the state animal. The helmet of a knight's suit of armor faces forward, representing sovereignty for a state that governs itself. Below the helmet is a shield with three plows on it. The plows show the importance of agriculture to the state's economic power.

   Two female figures are pictured in the state seal. Liberty on the left, carries the liberty cap on her staff. Colonial patriots wore the liberty cap as a symbol of rebellion. Ceres, the Roman goddess of grain, is on the right. She holds a cornucopia filled with harvested produce, symbolizing abundance. Below it all is a banner with the state's motto, "Liberty and Prosperity."

READ ABOUT

The Thomas Alva Edison Memorial Tower was built on Edison's 91st birthday as a tribute to his inventions and accomplishments.

ECONOMY

★

I N 1876, THE FIRST RESEARCH AND DEVELOPMENT LABORATORY IN THE WORLD OPENED AT MENLO PARK, NEW JERSEY. This town has since been renamed Edison, in honor of the man who set up this laboratory. Thomas Alva Edison called it his "invention factory," and he worked there until 1887, when he moved to larger quarters in nearby West Orange. At Menlo Park, Edison invented the phonograph and the first practical electric lightbulb.

SEE IT HERE!

MENLO PARK

Today, the Menlo Park Museum and Tower stand on the site of Thomas Edison's original lab. Here you can see Edison's early phonograph and lightbulb, his motion-picture camera, his telegraphic equipment, and dozens of other inventions. The tower on the grounds is a memorial to Edison, a genius who transformed life on Earth.

WORKING IN NEW JERSEY

Now there are hundreds of laboratories in New Jersey. There are also factories and farms, hospitals and universities, hotels and restaurants, and shops and parks. More than 80 percent of all New Jerseyans work in the service industries. People in the service industries provide services to others. A waiter who dishes out ice cream on the boardwalk is working in the service industry. So is a brain surgeon at University Hospital in Newark, a professor at Princeton, and an insurance salesperson from Short Hills.

Tourism is one of the most important parts of New Jersey's service economy. Banking, insurance, and real estate are among the state's other major service industries. Food service, health care, teaching, and retail sales also fall in to that category.

This restaurant owner fills a take-out order in a Morristown eatery.

THE SILVER SCREEN

In 1908, people all over the United States were discovering a new kind of entertainment: the motion picture. While an organist played stirring music, actors pranced silently across the screen. Most of those early silent movies were filmed in New Jersey. Moviemaking is one of the many industries that sprang up in the Garden State. In the years since, the state has provided the backdrop for countless films, including *Confessions of a Teenage Drama Queen* (2004) and *Superman Returns* (2006).

The term "cliff-hanger" comes from a series of silent movies called the *Perils of Pauline*. In one, Pauline hangs by her hands from the steep Palisades overlooking the Hudson River.

What Do New Jerseyans Do?

This color-coded chart shows what industries New Jerseyans work in.

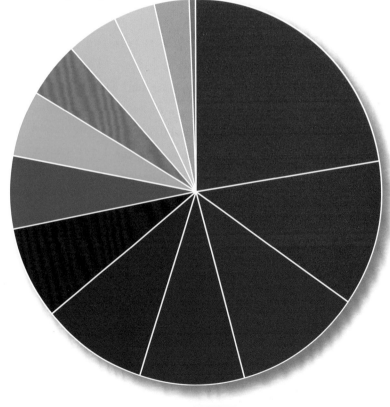

22.6% Educational services, and health care and social assistance, 953,449

12.3% Professional, scientific, and management, and administrative and waste management services, 519,327

11.1% Retail trade, 469,686

9.2% Manufacturing, 388,520

9.1% Finance and insurance, and real estate and rental and leasing, 382,392

7.9% Arts, entertainment, and recreation, and accommodation and food services, 332,171

5.9% Construction, 249,241

5.7% Transportation and warehousing, and utilities, 241,784

4.6% Public administration, 195,598

4.4% Other services, except public administration, 187,517

3.7% Wholesale trade, 154,917

3.1% Information, 131,703

0.4% Agriculture, forestry, fishing and hunting, and mining, 15,078

Source: U.S. Census Bureau, 2010 census

SETH BOYDEN: THE INVENTOR FROM NEWARK

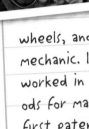

As a boy in Massachusetts, Seth Boyden (1788–1870) loved to take apart clocks and watches. By studying timepieces, he taught himself a lot about springs, wheels, and gears. Soon he became an excellent mechanic. In 1813, he moved to Newark, where he worked in the leather business. He invented methods for making patent leather and opened the first patent leather factory in the United States. But he didn't stop there. He went on to discover new ways to make cast iron. He built locomotives and improved the steam engine. He even got interested in growing strawberries and developed a delicious new variety. Thomas Edison later called Boyden one of the greatest inventors in the United States.

? **Want to know more?** Visit www.factsfornow .scholastic.com and enter the keywords **New Jersey**.

WORD TO KNOW

pharmaceutical *having to do with medicinal drugs*

MADE IN NEW JERSEY

In the past, New Jersey's cities were forests of factory smokestacks. But in the late 20th century, that picture changed. Today, only about 9 percent of all New Jerseyans work in manufacturing.

Manufacturing is still important there, however. New Jersey is a leading state in the chemical industry. Several giant **pharmaceutical** companies have headquarters in New Jersey. These include Johnson & Johnson, Merck, and Hoffmann-La Roche. Other chemical products made in New Jersey are shampoos, cosmetics, soaps, paints, and plastics.

Did you ever wonder who puts pears and peaches into the cans you see on the supermarket shelves? There's a good chance that the canning was done in New Jersey. Fruit and vegetable canning are major industries in and around Camden.

The glassmaking industry uses tons of sand, and sand is plentiful in southern New Jersey. Glassmaking is big business in Vineland, Millville, and Bridgeton. Factories in this area turn out bottles, windowpanes, and scientific equipment such as test tubes.

Major Agricultural and Mining Products

This map shows where New Jersey's major agricultural and mining products come from. See a tree? That means nursery products are found there.

Top Products

Manufacturing   Chemicals, food and beverages, medical equipment, computer and electronic products, fabricated metal products, plastics and rubber products

Agriculture   Greenhouse products, blueberries, horses and mules, corn, peaches, soybeans

Mining   Sand and gravel, traprock

Fisheries   Scallops, clams, crabs

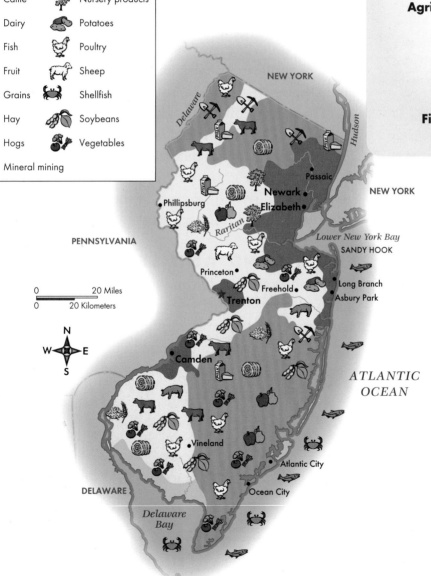

Legend:
- Cattle
- Dairy
- Fish
- Fruit
- Grains
- Hay
- Hogs
- Mineral mining
- Nursery products
- Potatoes
- Poultry
- Sheep
- Shellfish
- Soybeans
- Vegetables

NEW YORK

PENNSYLVANIA

Delaware

Phillipsburg

Raritan

Passaic

Newark

Elizabeth

NEW YORK

Lower New York Bay

SANDY HOOK

Hudson

Princeton

Freehold

Trenton

Long Branch

Asbury Park

0   20 Miles
0   20 Kilometers

N W E S

Camden

ATLANTIC OCEAN

Vineland

Atlantic City

DELAWARE

Ocean City

Delaware Bay

The New Jersey Department of Agriculture is working to promote horticultural businesses in the state.

REAPING THE HARVEST

Only about 1 percent of the people in the Garden State work in farming today. Still, one-sixth of New Jersey's land is used for agriculture. Altogether, New Jersey has about 9,900 farms.

Roses for corsages, lilies and orchids for flower arrangements, poinsettia plants for the holidays—all are grown in New Jersey's greenhouses. Greenhouse farming is especially important in northeastern New Jersey. Small vegetable farms are scattered throughout the state. New Jersey farmers raise asparagus, bell peppers, eggplants, spinach, cabbages, snap beans, and sweet corn.

The sandy soil of the Pine Barrens is excellent for raising blueberries and cranberries. Southern New Jersey also has apple and peach orchards.

Dairy cows graze in New Jersey's northwestern hills. Dairy farms are found farther south, as well, in Salem and Burlington counties.

FROM LAND AND SEA

Sand and gravel beds throughout New Jersey supply materials for the construction industry. Peat and greensand marl, used in fertilizers, are mined in central New Jersey. Granite comes from quarries in the northwest.

We're Proud to Offer

JERSEY GROWN

FROM THE GARDEN STATE

When it comes to beautiful, healthy flowers, plants, trees and shrubs, nobody does it better than New Jersey's growers.

Jersey Grown is:
• Accustomed to New Jersey's soil and growing conditions
• Checked for quality
• Disease and pest-free

New Jersey Department of Agriculture, Charles M. Kuperus, Secretary

Some of the richest clam beds stretch along the east coast, from Barnegat Bay to Cape May. Clams, lobsters, blue crabs, and squids are harvested off the New Jersey shore each year. Commercial fishing boats bring in flounder, menhaden, and swordfish.

KEEPING IN TOUCH

New Jersey's history in the communications field reaches all the way back to the 1830s. The world's first telegraph message was tapped out at an old iron mill in Morristown on January 6, 1838. Using a code of dots and dashes, an engineer named Alfred Vail sent a message along 3 miles (4.8 km) of wire to his friend Samuel F. B. Morse. The simple message, "A patient waiter is no loser," launched the age of telecommunications.

New Jersey went on to make history with the telephone. The first interstate long-distance call was placed in 1877 between New Brunswick and New York City. In 1951, Englewood was the first town in the United States to pioneer direct-dial service. Bell Laboratories in Murray Hill designed the first satellite to be used for international broadcasting.

Today, New Jersey is working to be a leader in the telecommunications field. Tyco, Lucent, and Univision are among the dozens of communications companies that have headquarters in the state. New Jersey keeps people talking to one another!

FAQ

Q8 WHAT WAS THE FIRST RADIO SIGNAL BROADCAST?

A8 In 1840, Joseph Henry, a professor at Princeton, sent the sound of a bell from one campus building to another. Using primitive radio equipment, he had transmitted the world's first radio signal.

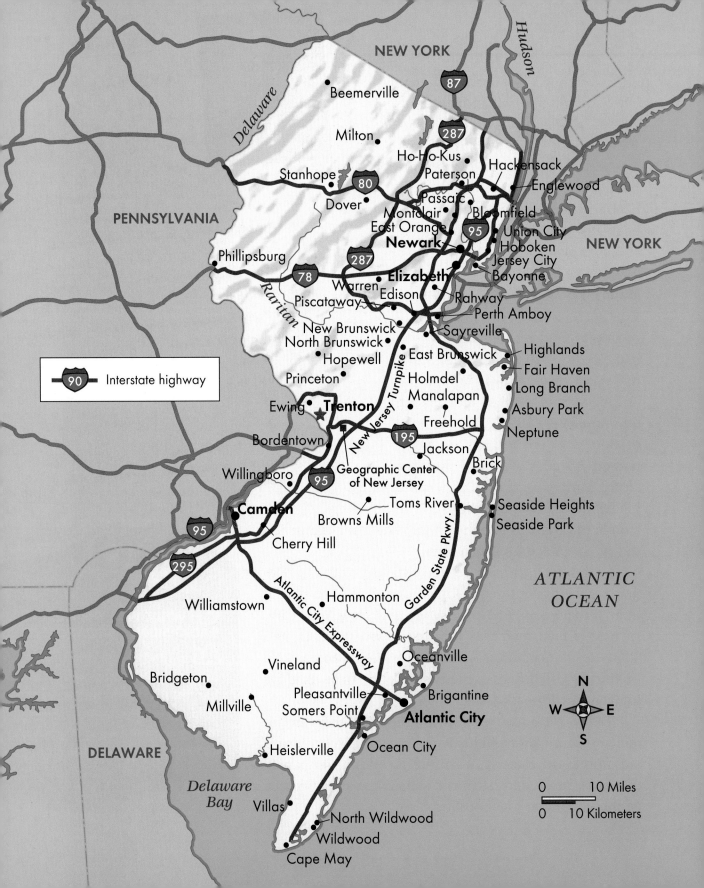

NEW YORK

Hudson

Delaware

Beemerville

Milton

Ho-Ho-Kus

Hackensack

87

Stanhope

Paterson

Englewood

80

Dover

Passaic

Bloomfield

PENNSYLVANIA

Montclair

East Orange

95

Union City

Newark

Hoboken

Jersey City

Phillipsburg

Elizabeth

Bayonne

287

78

Warren

Edison

Rahway

NEW YORK

Piscataway

Perth Amboy

New Brunswick

Sayreville

North Brunswick

Highlands

Hopewell

East Brunswick

Fair Haven

Princeton

Holmdel

Long Branch

| 90 | Interstate highway |

Manalapan

Asbury Park

Ewing

Trenton

Freehold

Neptune

Bordentown

195

Jackson

Brick

Willingboro

Geographic Center of New Jersey

95

Camden

Toms River

Seaside Heights

Browns Mills

Seaside Park

Cherry Hill

95

295

Hammonton

ATLANTIC OCEAN

Williamstown

Oceanville

Vineland

Bridgeton

Brigantine

Pleasantville

Millville

Somers Point

Atlantic City

N

DELAWARE

Heislerville

Ocean City

W   E

S

Delaware Bay

Villas

0   10 Miles

North Wildwood

0   10 Kilometers

Wildwood

Cape May

Raritan

New Jersey Turnpike

Atlantic City Expressway

Garden State Pkwy.

CHAPTER NINE

TRAVEL GUIDE

TRAVEL GUIDE

★

YOU CAN LEARN A LOT ABOUT NEW JERSEY FROM BOOKS AND WEB SITES. And you can learn even more by seeing it for yourself. Discover New Jersey wildlife by taking a leisurely stroll down one of the state's many pristine beaches or study its economy on one of its bustling boardwalks. Enjoy local attractions such as theme parks, horse racing, and whale watching, or learn about the state's history at the capital city of Trenton.

← Follow along with this travel map. We'll begin in Trenton and travel all the way down to Cape May!

DELAWARE RIVER

THINGS TO DO: Learn about local government, tour an Ivy League university, and visit an aquarium.

Trenton

★ **New Jersey State House:** This is the second-oldest capitol in continuous use in the United States. The governor's wing dates from 1792. Step into the legislative quarters, which have been restored to their turn-of-the-century splendor, and see where elected representatives make decisions for New Jersey.

★ **New Jersey State Museum:** At this museum you'll find porcelains from New Jersey's historic ceramic industry and a descriptive map of major battles fought in New Jersey. And you can learn all about the solar system and space exploration through virtual recreations and sky shows at the museum's planetarium.

★ **Patriots Theater at the War Memorial:** Ballet, comedy, and music of all styles are performed on this historic stage.

★ **Abbott Farm National Historic Landmark:** See where archaeologists learned about New Jersey's amazing history. Some archaeological sites date back to the colonial era and even as far back as 8000 BCE.

New Jersey State Museum

Camden

★ **Adventure Aquarium:** The West African River Experience features hippopotamuses, crocodiles, porcupines, and more than 20 species of African birds in a free-flight aviary. Be sure to visit the 4D Theatre, which features films with marine-life themes.

★ **Camden Children's Garden:** This 4-acre (1.6 ha) garden has something for everyone. The Storybook Garden features gardens inspired by popular children's stories. Be sure to stop by the whimsical Alice in Wonderland Garden which features the Queen of Hearts chair. At the Butterfly Garden, get a firsthand look at the relationship between butterflies and plants.

Clementon

★ **Clementon Amusement Park & Splash World:** Beat the summer heat on the Sky River Rapids slide, which features three sets of slides and three huge splash pools. Six lanes of competitive head-first mat racing start with a swift drop at the top on the Vertical Limit Racer slide. Relax on the Lazy River or get soaked at Pirates Cove.

An English literature class at Princeton University

Princeton

★ **Princeton University:** Take a tour of this historic campus. Chartered in 1746 as the College of New Jersey, today's Princeton University is a member of the elite Ivy League conference, which also includes Harvard, Yale, Brown, Columbia, Dartmouth, the University of Pennsylvania, and Cornell.

SEE IT HERE!

HOWELL LIVING HISTORY FARM

If you travel to Titusville, be sure to make time for the Howell Living History Farm. You'll learn about farming circa 1900. Check out sheep shearing and maple sugaring. Or take a hayride! The farm specializes in catering to kids and school groups.

GATEWAY

THINGS TO DO: Learn about the history of aviation, see world-class performers sing, dance, and act, or see where many immigrants first entered the United States.

MINI-BIO

MORRIS FRANK: GOING TO THE DOGS

After he lost his sight at age 16, Morris Frank (1908–1975) felt helpless and discouraged. Then he learned that dogs were being trained in Europe to guide blinded veterans. He offered to help launch a similar program in the United States. He went to Switzerland to get his first dog guide, a German shepherd named Buddy. With Buddy by his side, Frank returned home and helped start The Seeing Eye in 1929. In 1930, The Seeing Eye moved to spacious grounds in Morristown, New Jersey. There the school carries on the legacy of Morris Frank. The Seeing Eye has helped thousands of blind men and women gain independence through partnership with a dog guide.

? **Want to know more?** Visit www.factsfornow .scholastic.com and enter the keywords **New Jersey**.

Jersey City

★ **Liberty Island:** The Statue of Liberty, or Lady Liberty, resides on her own island. Tours of the grounds are offered throughout the day and feature views of the statue, as well as New York Harbor. Don't miss the Statue of Liberty exhibit, which chronicles the history of one of the most recognizable symbols of freedom.

★ **Ellis Island:** This island was the first stop for many European immigrants to the United States during the waves of immigration in the 19th and 20th centuries. The Ellis Island Immigration Museum features photographs, videos, and exhibits on the immigrant experience at Ellis Island and its overall place in U.S. immigration history. Don't miss the American Immigrant Wall of Honor, the world's longest wall of names and a special tribute to American immigration.

The Statue of Liberty

The Ballantine House at the Newark Museum

Newark

★ **New Jersey Performing Arts Center:** Take in a concert, a dance performance, or a musical at this stunning theater, which opened in 1997. The New Jersey Symphony Orchestra often performs there, and other performers have included the Alvin Ailey American Dance Theater, Liza Minnelli, and Yo-Yo Ma. Guided tours offer visitors a look at several aspects of the center, including backstage areas.

★ **New Jersey Historical Society:** This museum dedicates itself to all aspects of New Jersey's history. The library houses an impressive collection of manuscripts and photographs dating as far back as the colonial era. You're sure to learn something new through informative exhibits, including an exhibit on the state's relationship to rivers throughout its history.

★ **Newark Museum:** This museum complex is the largest in New Jersey. It has 80 galleries of art and science. Galleries feature art from all over the world and include Asian, Latin American, Native American, and African collections. Visit the Mini Zoo to observe 50 animal species and learn about their natural habitats.

SEE IT HERE!

RUTGERS UNIVERSITY

Rutgers University is one of the nation's top-ranked public universities. And you can visit its largest campus in New Brunswick/Piscataway. Check out the Jane Voorhees Zimmerli Art Museum, which has exhibits of Russian and Soviet art, as well as French and American prints and a rare book collection. Or make a stop at the New Jersey Museum of Agriculture or the East Asian Library.

Atlantic City Boardwalk

West Orange

★ **Edison National Historic Site:** Come and see Edison's historic invention factory, laboratory, and workshops where he developed the phonograph and the motion picture camera.

Teterboro

★ **Aviation Hall of Fame and Museum of New Jersey:** Want to learn about New Jersey's aeronautical history? This is the place! Visitors can view air and space equipment, as well as photographs and fine art collections.

HOW DID BOARDWALKS GET STARTED?

In 1870, a hotel owner in Atlantic City got tired of guests tracking sand through his lobby. A railroad conductor named Alex Boardman suggested building a wooden walkway over the beach. Some say that the first boardwalk was called Boardman's Walk.

GREATER ATLANTIC CITY

THINGS TO DO: Enjoy a walk on the boardwalk, learn about civil rights, or see the world's tallest elephant!

Atlantic City

★ **Atlantic City Boardwalk:** Internationally known as the world's first boardwalk, this boardwalk was built in 1870. It is lined with shops and restaurants, and even has places to skateboard. Check out Atlantic City Boardwalk Arcade, one of the largest arcades in Atlantic City.

Most of the names on the Monopoly game board come from places in Atlantic City.

★ **Civil Rights Garden:** Walk through the Civil Rights Garden, which honors the history and important figures of the civil rights movement. You can read bits of Martin Luther King's famous speeches and writings posted in the garden.

★ **Ripley's Believe It or Not! Museum:** See strange and unusual exhibits from Robert Ripley's travels, as well as films and an interactive fun house. You'll see a collection of shrunken heads and a roulette wheel made entirely of jellybeans!

★ **Absecon Lighthouse:** You can take in the view from atop the historic Absecon Lighthouse. Built in 1857, this 171-foot (52-m) tower was built under the supervision of George Gordon Meade.

Lucy the Elephant

Margate

★ **Lucy the Elephant:** Come see the tallest elephant in the world! The 65-foot-high (20-m) wooden elephant was constructed in 1881. Tours are offered several times throughout the day. You won't want to miss this great photo op!

Oceanville

★ **Edwin B. Forsythe National Wildlife Refuge:** Experience the ultimate outdoors hike through this 42,000-acre (17,000-ha) refuge. Glimpse local wildlife, including a large variety of bird species, and walk through beautiful natural trails. You may see turtles sunning themselves or you may spot an eagle soaring overhead!

Somers Point

★ **Atlantic County Historical Society:** This facility offers genealogical records and early photos from the local area's history. The museum has an impressive collection of historical objects, including examples of clothing from the Victorian era.

Absecon Lighthouse

SHORE

THINGS TO DO: Enjoy a view from atop a beautiful lighthouse, visit a famous fort, or take a ride on a unique carousel.

Highlands

★ **Twin-Lights Navesink Lighthouse Historic Site:** Enjoy stunning sights at 256 feet (78 m) above the water in this two-beacon lighthouse, which overlooks Sandy Hook and the Atlantic Ocean.

★ **Fort Hancock:** This fort is located in the Sandy Hook region of Gateway National Recreation Area, near the tip of the Sandy Hook peninsula. It overlooks the entrance to New York Harbor. Fort Hancock has played a key role

in harbor defense and navigation since 1764 when the Sandy Hook Lighthouse (the oldest operating lighthouse in America) was built.

Seaside Heights

★ **Floyd Moreland Historic Dentzel/Looff Carousel:** Go round and round on this classic antique carousel. Built about 1910, it is one of two American-crafted, hand-carved antique carousels in New Jersey.

Reenactment of the Battle of Monmouth

Manalapan

★ **Monmouth Battlefield State Park:** See the Revolutionary War's Battle of Monmouth reenacted every June. Visitors can also enjoy miles of hiking and horseback riding trails, or have a relaxing picnic.

Marathon runners at the Sandy Hook Lighthouse

Jackson

★ **Six Flags Hurricane Harbor:**
Take a thrilling roller coaster ride,
chug along the Scenic Railway or
catch a colorful stage show at Six
Flags Great America theme park.
And if you don't like roller coast-
ers, take a splash at the Hurricane
Harbor Water Park.

★ **Prospertown Schoolhouse:** This
150-year-old one-room schoolhouse
contains photographs, artifacts, and
documents telling the history of
Jackson.

Holmdel

★ **David C. Shaw Arboretum:** Take
a tour through this garden and see
beautiful trees and flowering plant
life.

★ **New Jersey Vietnam Veterans'
Memorial Foundation &
Vietnam Era Educational
Center:** This memorial honors the
New Jerseyans who served in the
Vietnam War. The center features
exhibits that explore the history of
the Vietnam conflict.

SKYLANDS

THINGS TO DO: Take a
journey back in time to the
Wild West, or relive the rich
history of the American railroad.

Phillipsburg

★ **Phillipsburg Railroad Historians
Museum:** Do you love trains?
Check out a great display of rail-
road memorabilia and artifacts.
There's even a replica of an exist-
ing steam railroad line.

Beemerville

★ **Space Farms Zoo and Museum:**
The zoo houses more than 100
different species of animals. The
museum has a variety of exhibits
on several aspects of American history. Don't miss the Eskimo exhibit
or the collection of antique cars
and motorcycles.

Stanhope

★ **Wild West City:** This theme park focuses on all things Western. Live-action shows bring the glory days of the cowboy to life in a setting inspired by the Old West. Highlights include a petting zoo, train, stagecoach, and pony rides.

SEE IT HERE!

LAKOTA WOLF PRESERVE

Do you thrill to the sound of a wolf howling in the mountains? If you do, check out the Lakota Wolf Preserve in Warren County. There you can watch and listen to packs of timber, tundra, and arctic wolves in their natural surroundings. You'll also see bobcats and foxes in the reserve.

Ogdensburg

★ **Sterling Hill Mining Museum:** Sterling Hill Mine was the last operating mine in New Jersey when it closed in 1986. Today, the museum offers tours of this world famous zinc mine.

The National Marbles Tournament

SOUTHERN SHORE

THINGS TO DO: Learn about the game of marbles, explore Native American history, or take in a play.

Wildwood

★ **George F. Boyer Historical Museum:** This museum features old photographs and artifacts depicting the history of Wildwood from the distant past to the present.

★ **National Marbles Hall of Fame:** This museum, housed in the George F. Boyer Historical Museum, displays the history of the National Marble Tournament that takes place each year in Wildwood.

★ **Splash Zone Water Park:** Voted by some as the "Best Water Park," this place is an interactive water park for every member of the family. Visitors can thrill to the blazing velocity of the Speed Dominator or relax their way down Adventure River. For very young children there's Zoe Zone, a water park playground.

Bridgeton

★ **Woodruff Museum of Indian Artifacts:** This museum features more than 30,000 artifacts from the Lenni-Lenape Indians of New Jersey, including axes, arrowheads, and pottery.

Heislerville

★ **East Point Lighthouse:** Climb atop this beautiful lighthouse, situated on Delaware Bay. Built in 1849, this lighthouse has guided boaters into the mouth of the Maurice River for generations.

Cape May is the oldest seashore resort in the United States. It dates back to 1761.

Cape May

★ **Cape May Lighthouse:** Located at Cape May Point State Park, the lighthouse is 157 feet (48 m) high. It was built in 1859 and is still an aid to navigation. Visitors who climb the 199 steps are rewarded with a panoramic view of the Cape May peninsula.

★ **Cape May Stage:** Come see a hilarious comedy, a thrilling musical, or a classic American drama. Founded in 1988, the stage hosts great performances in a cozy space.

★ **Emlen Physick Estate:** Built in 1879 by renowned architect Frank Furness, this house now serves as a Victorian museum. Take a guided tour of the mansion's interior, filled with original Victorian furniture and architectural details. Don't forget to have tea in the carriage house!

Cape May Lighthouse

WRITING PROJECTS

Check out these ideas for creating a campaign brochure and writing you-are-there editorials. Or research the migration paths of settlers and explorers.

118

ART PROJECTS

Build a Lenape wigwam, create a great PowerPoint presentation, or learn about the state quarter and design your own.

119

TIMELINE

What happened when? This timeline highlights important events in the state's history—and shows what was happening throughout the United States at the same time.

122

FAST FACTS

Use this section to find fascinating facts about state symbols, land area and population statistics, weather, sports teams, and much more.

126

GLOSSARY

Remember the Words to Know from the chapters in this book? They're all collected here.

125

SCIENCE, TECHNOLOGY, ENGINEERING, & MATH PROJECTS

Make weather maps, graph population statistics, and research endangered species that live in the state.

120

PRIMARY VS. SECONDARY SOURCES

121

So what are primary and secondary sources and what's the diff? This section explains all that and where you can find them.

BIOGRAPHICAL DICTIONARY

This at-a-glance guide highlights some of the state's most important and influential people. Visit this section and read about their contributions to the state, the country, and the world.

133

RESOURCES

Books and much more. Take a look at these additional sources for information about the state.

138

WRITING PROJECTS

Create an Election Brochure or Web Site!

Run for office!

In this book, you've read about some of the issues that concern New Jersey today. As a candidate for governor of New Jersey, create a campaign brochure or Web site. Explain how you meet the qualifications to be governor of New Jersey and talk about the three or four major issues you'll focus on if you are elected. Remember, you'll be responsible for New Jersey's budget! How would you spend the taxpayers' money?
SEE: Chapter Seven, pages 90–92.

Write a Memoir, Journal, or Editorial for Your School Newspaper!

Picture Yourself . . .

★ as a Lenape growing up in northern New Jersey before the arrival of the Europeans.
SEE: Chapter Two, pages 24–33.

★ as a young patriot in the days before the American Revolution. Write a letter to the newspaper, explaining why the Greenwich Tea Party was necessary.
SEE: Chapter Three, pages 44–45.

Compare and Contrast—When, Why, and How Did They Come?

Compare the migration and explorations of the first Native people and the first Europeans. Tell about:

1. When their migrations began
2. How they traveled
3. Why they migrated
4. Where their journeys began and ended
5. What they found when they arrived

SEE: Chapters Two and Three, pages 25–29, 35–39.

ART PROJECTS

Create a PowerPoint Presentation or Visitors' Guide

Welcome to New Jersey!

New Jersey is a great place to visit and to live! From its natural beauty to its bustling cities and historic sites, there's plenty to see and do. In your PowerPoint presentation or brochure, highlight 10 to 15 of New Jersey's amazing landmarks. Be sure to include:

★ a map of the state showing where these sites are located

★ photos, illustrations, Web links, natural history facts, geographic stats, climate and weather, plants and wildlife, recent discoveries

SEE: Chapter One, pages 19–21; Chapter Nine, pages 105–115.

Build a Lenape Wigwam or Longhouse

During the summer months, the Lenape often lived in wigwams, or tents made of animal skins. They lived in longhouses during the winter. What do you need to build a wigwam or longhouse?

SEE: Chapter Two, pages 29–30

State Quarter Project

From 1999 to 2008, the U.S. Mint introduced new quarters commemorating each of the 50 states in the order that they were admitted to the Union. Each state's quarter features a unique design on its back, or reverse.

★ Go to www.factsfornow.scholastic.com and enter the keywords **New Jersey**. Look for the link to the New Jersey quarter to find out what's featured on the back. (Here's a hint: History played a big part in what was chosen for the design!)

★ Research the significance of each image. Who designed the quarter? Who chose the final design?

★ Design your own New Jersey quarter. What images would you choose for the reverse?

★ Make a poster showing the New Jersey quarter and label each image.

SCIENCE, TECHNOLOGY, ENGINEERING, & MATH PROJECTS

Track Endangered Species

Using your knowledge of New Jersey's wildlife, research which animals and plants are endangered or threatened.

★ Find out what the state is doing to protect these species.

★ Chart known populations of the animals and plants, and report on changes in certain geographical areas.

SEE: Chapter One, page 21.

A red-shouldered hawk

Graph Population Trends!

★ Compare population statistics (such as ethnic background, birth, death, and literacy rates) in New Jersey counties or major cities.

★ In your graph or chart, look at population density and write sentences describing what the population statistics show; graph one set of population statistics and write a paragraph explaining what the graphs reveal.

SEE: Chapter Six, pages 72–74.

Create a Weather Map of New Jersey!

Use your knowledge of New Jersey's geography to research and identify conditions that result in specific weather events. What is it about the geography of New Jersey that makes it vulnerable to certain types of weather? Make a weather map or poster that shows the weather patterns over the state. To accompany your map, explain the technology used to measure weather phenomena and provide data.

SEE: Chapter One, pages 17–18.

PRIMARY VS. SECONDARY SOURCES

What's the Diff?

Your teacher may require at least one or two primary sources and one or two secondary sources for your assignment. So, what's the difference between the two?

★ **Primary sources are original.** You are reading the actual words of someone's diary, journal, letter, autobiography or interview. Primary sources can also be photographs, maps, prints, cartoons, news/film footage, posters, first-person newspaper articles, drawings, musical scores, and recordings. By the way, when you conduct a survey, interview someone, shoot a video, or take photographs to include in a project—you are creating primary sources!

★ **Secondary sources are what you find in encyclopedias, textbooks, articles, biographies, and almanacs.** These are written by a person or group of people who tell about something that happened to someone else. Secondary sources also recount what another person said or did. This book is an example of a secondary source.

Now that you know what primary sources are—where can you find them?

★ **Your school or local library:** Check the library catalog for collections of original writings, government documents, musical scores, and so on. Some of this material may be stored on microfilm.

★ **Historical societies:** These organizations keep historical documents, photographs, and other materials. Staff members can help you find what you are looking for. History museums are also great places to see primary sources firsthand.

★ **The Internet:** There are lots of sites that have primary sources you can download and use in a project or assignment.

A letter from Abraham Lincoln, 1861

TIMELINE

★ ★ ★

U.S. Events `1500` **New Jersey Events**

1524
Giovanni da Verrazzano anchors briefly off Sandy Hook; he is probably the first European to sight the coast of present-day New Jersey.

`1600`

1607
The first permanent English settlement is established in North America at Jamestown.

1609
Henry Hudson sails up the Hudson River under the Dutch flag.

1618
Dutch traders set up a trading post at Bergen, the first European settlement in present-day New Jersey.

1620
Pilgrims found Plymouth Colony, the second permanent English settlement.

1623
Cornelis Mey, a Dutch captain, explores Cape May and Delaware Bay.

1629
Dutch settlers establish Pavonia (present-day Jersey City).

James, Duke of York

1638
Swedish colonists establish a small settlement on the New Jersey side of Delaware Bay.

1664
England's King Charles II sends his navy to seize New Netherland from the Dutch; area is renamed after the Isle of Jersey and given to the Duke of York.

1682
René-Robert Cavelier, Sieur de La Salle, claims more than 1 million square miles (2.6 million sq km) of territory in the Mississippi River basin for France, naming it Louisiana.

1665
Lord John Berkeley and Sir George Carteret become proprietors of New Jersey and split the colony into East Jersey and West Jersey.

U.S. Events `1700` **New Jersey Events**

1702
East Jersey and West Jersey are
united to form a single colony.

1755–63
England and France fight over North
American colonial lands in the French
and Indian War. By the end of the
war, France has ceded all of its land
west of the Mississippi to Spain and
its Canadian territories to England.

1758
Brotherton is established as the first
Indian reservation in America.

1774
Angry colonists in Greenwich burn a shipment
of British tea in an event called the Greenwich
Tea Party.

1776
Thirteen American colonies declare their
independence from Britain, marking the
beginning of the Revolutionary War.

1776
On December 26, Washington crosses the
Delaware to surprise the Hessian soldiers at Trenton.

1778
On June 28, the British and Continental
armies clash in the Battle of Monmouth.

1787
The U.S. Constitution is written.

1787
New Jersey is the third state to
ratify the U.S. Constitution.

1803 `1800`
The Louisiana Purchase almost doubles
the size of the United States.

1804
Vice President Aaron Burr kills Alexander Hamilton
in a duel at Weehawken; New Jersey passes
a law regarding the gradual ending of slavery.

1812–15
The United States and Britain
fight the War of 1812.

1830
The Indian Removal Act forces eastern
Native American groups to relocate
west of the Mississippi River.

1836
The Morris Canal crosses New Jersey
from Phillipsburg to Jersey City, linking
the Delaware and Hudson rivers.

1846–48
The United States fights a war with Mexico
over western territories in the Mexican War.

1865
The last slaves are freed in New Jersey.

U.S. Events

1898
The United States gains control of Cuba, Puerto Rico, the Philippines, and Guam after defeating Spain in the Spanish-American War.

1917-18
The United States engages in World War I.

1929
The stock market crashes, plunging the United States into the Great Depression.

1941-45
The United States engages in World War II.

1991
The United States and other nations fight the brief Persian Gulf War against Iraq.

2001
Terrorists hijack four U.S. aircraft and crash them into the World Trade Center in New York City, the Pentagon in Washington, D.C., and a Pennsylvania field, killing thousands.

New Jersey Events

1873
Poet Walt Whitman moves to Camden and becomes the center of a literary community.

`1900`

1913
Silk workers in Paterson strike for five months for better working conditions.

1927
The Holland Tunnel opens, joining Jersey City with Lower Manhattan.

1931
The George Washington Bridge opens to traffic.

1967
Newark erupts in riots, leaving 26 people dead and causing $10,000,000 in property damage.

1970
Kenneth Gibson becomes Newark's first African American mayor.

1976
Casino gambling is legalized in Atlantic City; the Meadowlands Sports Complex opens.

1978
The federal government protects the Pinelands as the Pinelands National Reserve.

1997
The first concert is held at the New Jersey Center for the Performing Arts in Newark.

`2000`

2012
Hurricane Sandy slams New Jersey, killing 37 people.

The boardwalk at Atlantic City

GLOSSARY

★ ★ ★

abolish to put an end to

archaeologist a person who studies the remains of past human societies

barrier islands islands that are created by the gradual buildup of sand and stones from the ocean floor

commuters people who travel to and from work, often from suburbs to cities

corrupt characterized by immoral and illegal actions

discrimination unequal treatment based on race, gender, religion, or other factor

emancipation the act of freeing people from slavery or other control

famine period of extreme food shortages and hunger

fraud cheating and lying

fugitive someone who is trying to escape or is on the run

glacier a slowly moving sheet of ice

immunity natural protection against disease

indentured servants people who work for others under contract

infamous famously terrible

marl type of clay containing lime in the form of fossil shells

mediate help opposing sides reach an agreement

military draft requirement that all eligible persons must register for duty in the armed forces

pharmaceutical having to do with medicinal drugs

radioactive giving off atomic particles, which can be dangerous to living things

ratify approve

reform to clean up or improve

repealed withdrew; undid

segregation separation based on race, gender, religion, or other factor

sinews tendons of an animal that can be used as cord or thread

strike an organized refusal to work, usually to protest wages or working conditions

Tories people who remained loyal to the British during the American Revolution

toxic waste leftover material from factories that can be poisonous

wampum belts belts that were made by stringing together many round, flat seashells

FAST FACTS

★ ★ ★

State Symbols

Statehood date	December 18, 1787, the 3rd state
Origin of state name	Named by the Duke of York after England's Isle of Jersey
State capital	Trenton
State nickname	Garden State
State motto	"Liberty and Prosperity"
State bird	Eastern goldfinch
State flower	Common violet
State dinosaur	*Hadrosaurus foulkii*
State animal	Horse
State shell	Knobbed whelk
State folk dance	Square dance
State song	"I'm from New Jersey" (see p.128 for lyrics)
State tree	Red oak
State fair	Sussex County (August)

State seal

Geography

Total area; rank	8,721 square miles (22,587 sq km); 47th
Land; rank	7,417 square miles (19,210 sq km); 46th
Water; rank	1,304 square miles (3,377 sq km); 27th
Inland water; rank	396 square miles (1,026 sq km); 38th
Coastal waters; rank	401 square miles (1,039 sq km); 14th
Territorial waters; rank	507 square miles (1,313 sq km); 13th
Geographic center	Mercer County, 5 miles (8 km) southeast of Trenton
Latitude	38° 55' N to 41° 21' 23" N
Longitude	73° 53' 39" W to 75° 35' W
Highest point	High Point, 1,803 feet (550 m)
Lowest point	Sea level along Atlantic Ocean
Largest city	Newark
Number of counties	21
Longest river	Raritan, 75 miles (121 km)

Population

Population; rank (2010 census)	8,791,894; 11th
Density (2010 census)	1,185 persons per square mile (458 per sq km)
Population distribution (2010 census)	95% urban, 5% rural
Ethnic distribution (2010 census)	White persons: 59.3%
	Black or African American Persons: 12.8%
	Asian Persons: 8.2%
	American Indian and Alaska Native persons: 0.1%
	Persons of two or more races: 1.5%
	Hispanic or Latino persons: 17.7%
	People of some other race: 0.3%

Weather

Record high temperature	110°F (43°C) at Runyon on July 10, 1936
Record low temperature	−34°F (−37°C) at River Vale on January 5, 1904
Average July temperature	75°F (24°C)
Average January temperature	31°F (−1°C)
Average yearly precipitation	40.6 inches (103.1 cm)

State flag

STATE SONG

★ ★ ★

"I'm from New Jersey"

Words and music by Red Mascara

New Jersey actually doesn't have an official song, but "I'm from New Jersey" is as close as it gets. It was written in 1961 by Red Mascara of Phillipsburg. This song passed both legislative houses in 1972. However, the governor did not sign it into law. It remains popular throughout the state.

I know of a state that's a perfect playland with white sandy beaches by the sea;
With fun-filled mountains, lakes and parks, and folks with hospitality;
With historic towns where battles were fought, and presidents have made their home;
It's called New Jersey, and I toast and tout it wherever I may roam. 'Cause . . .

(first chorus)
I'M FROM NEW JERSEY and I'm proud about it, I love the Garden State.
I'M FROM NEW JERSEY and I want to shout it, I think it's simply great.
All of the other states throughout the nation may mean a lot to some;
But I wouldn't want another, Jersey is like no other, I'm glad that's where I'm from.

(second chorus)
If you want glamour, try Atlantic City or Wildwood by the sea;
Then there is Trenton, Princeton, and Fort Monmouth, they all made history.
Each little town has got that certain something, from High Point to Cape May;
And some place like Mantoloking, Phillipsburg, or Hoboken will steal your heart away.

NATURAL AREAS AND HISTORIC SITES

★ ★ ★

National Scenic Trail

Appalachian Trail passes through the length of New Jersey. The trail is 2,158 miles (3,473 km) long and stretches from Maine to Georgia.

National Heritage Trail

New Jersey Coastal Heritage Trail Route is an auto trail stretching nearly 300 miles (480 km) along New Jersey's shore.

National Recreation Areas

Delaware Water Gap is a scenic and historic area along the New Jersey/Pennsylvania border.

Gateway National Recreation Area includes the nation's oldest operating lighthouse and forts that defended America earlier in its history.

National Scenic Rivers

Lower Delaware National Wild and Scenic River includes key portions of the largest free-flowing river in the eastern United States.

Great Egg Harbor National Scenic and Recreational River begins near Berlin, New Jersey and flows into the Atlantic Ocean.

National Historic Sites

New Jersey has two national historic sites including *Edison National Historic Site* (West Orange) which contains Thomas A. Edison's home, laboratories, and research facilities.

National Reserve

New Jersey Pinelands National Reserve is the country's first national reserve covering more than 1 million acres (405,000 ha) of farms, forests, and wetlands.

National Monuments

New Jersey has two national monuments including *Ellis Island National Monument* which preserves the site where more than 12 million immigrants entered the United States.

State Parks and Forest

New Jersey has 30 state parks, 11 state forests, 5 state marinas, and 5 state recreation areas.

SPORTS TEAMS

★ ★ ★

NCAA Teams (Division I)

Fairleigh Dickinson University *Knights*
Monmouth University *Hawks*
Princeton University *Tigers*
Rider University *Broncos*
Seton Hall University *Pirates*
St. Peter's College *Peacocks*
State University of New Jersey-Rutgers *Scarlet Knights*

PROFESSIONAL SPORTS TEAMS

★ ★ ★

National Basketball Association
New Jersey *Nets*

National Football League
New York *Jets*
New York *Giants*

National Hockey League
New Jersey *Devils*

CULTURAL INSTITUTIONS

★ ★ ★

Libraries

Harvey S. Firestone Library at Princeton University has the state's largest research collection.

Newark Public Library is the largest in the state.

State Library (Trenton) has a large law and history collection.

Museums

New Jersey State Museum (Trenton) features exhibits on archaeology, decorative arts, fine arts, and natural history.

Newark Museum includes a planetarium and art, science, and natural history exhibits.

The *National Headquarters of the Boy Scouts of America* has public exhibits devoted to the history of scouting in the United States.

Barnegat Lighthouse, on Long Beach Island, is a favorite subject of painters and photographers. The lighthouse is part of a state park that also includes a museum and a sandy beach.

Kean New Jersey State Aquarium, in Camden, features a tank with many kinds of fish, a seal pool, and a trout stream.

Waterloo Village, in Stanhope, is a restored village of the 1700s. The village includes a gristmill, blacksmith shops, and many furnished homes.

Performing Arts

The *New Jersey State Opera* (Clifton-Passaic) performs at the Aprea Theater in Clifton.

The *New Jersey Dance Theater Ensemble* (Westfield) performs ballet, modern, and contemporary dance programs.

Universities and Colleges

In 2011, New Jersey had 14 public and 30 private institutions of higher learning.

ANNUAL EVENTS

January–March

Annual Garden State Outdoor Sports Show in Edison (January)

Lambertville–New Hope Winter Festival (January)

George Washington's Birthday Celebration in Titusville (February)

April–June

Cherry Blossom Festival in Newark (April)

Shad Fest in Lambertville (April)

New Jersey State Chili and Salsa Cook-Off in Toms River (May)

Super Science Saturday in Trenton (May)

Annual Battle of Monmouth Reenactment in Manalapan (June)

ShopRite LPGA Classic in Somers Point (June)

National Marbles Tournament in Wildwood (June)

Whitesbog Blueberry Festival in Browns Mills (June)

Belmar Seafood Festival in Belmar (June)

Opera Festival in Princeton (June–July)

July–September

New Jersey Festival of Ballooning in Readington (July)

Hummingbird Extravaganza in Swainton (August)

Sussex Country Farm and Horse Show in Sussex (August)

October–December

Victorian Weekend in Cape May (October)

Chatsworth Cranberry Festival (October)

Reenactment of Washington's Crossing of the Delaware in Titusville (December 25)

Victorian Christmas Celebration in Cape May (December)

BIOGRAPHICAL DICTIONARY

Charles Conrad Abbott (1843–1919) was an archaeologist who discovered traces of early human inhabitants near his home outside Trenton.

Edwin Eugene "Buzz" Aldrin (1930–) is an astronaut who served as copilot under Neil Armstrong on the *Apollo 11* flight. On July 20, 1969, he became the second person ever to set foot on the moon. He was born in Cedarville.

Clara Barton (1821–1912) was a teacher who started a free school in Bordentown. She nursed soldiers during the Civil War and went on to found the American Red Cross.

William "Count" Basie (1904–1984) was a jazz pianist and composer. He made his first big-band recording in 1937. He was born in Red Bank.

Moe Berg (1902–1972) played baseball with the Brooklyn Dodgers, Chicago White Sox, and Boston Red Sox. He was also a scholar and linguist. During World War II, he was an American spy, posing as a German businessman. He was born in Newark.

Lawrence Peter "Yogi" Berra (1925–) was a professional baseball player and manager. He was named the American League's Most Valuable Player of the Year in 1951, 1954, and 1955. Beginning in 1946, he served 14 seasons as catcher with the New York Yankees. A longtime resident of Montclair, he won pennants as manager of both the Yankees and the Mets.

Judy Blume See page 83.

Jon Bon Jovi (1962–) grew up in Sayreville. He is the lead singer with the band Bon Jovi and also plays guitar and harmonica.

Seth Boyden See page 100.

Bill Bradley (1943–) served as U.S. senator from New Jersey from 1979 to 1997. Born in Missouri, he attended Princeton University.

Wendell Brooks See page 81.

Aaron Burr (1756–1836) was a statesman and adventurer. He served as vice president of the United States from 1801 to 1805. In 1804, he killed his longtime political rival, Alexander Hamilton, in a duel at Weehawken. He was born in Newark.

Grover Cleveland See page 92.

James Fenimore Cooper (1789–1851) is considered to be the first major novelist of the New World. He is best known for his Leatherstocking Tales, a series of novels about frontier life that include *The Last of the Mohicans*, *The Deerslayer*, and *The Pathfinder*. He was born in Burlington.

Edwin E. "Buzz" Aldrin

Jon Bon Jovi

Stephen Crane (1871–1900) was a novelist, short-story writer, and poet. He is best known for his novel about the Civil War, *The Red Badge of Courage*. He was born in Newark.

Dorothy Cross (1906–1972) was one of the first female archaeologists in the United States. She grew up in Trenton and she published a book on the Lenape called *The Indians of New Jersey*.

Victor Cruz (1986–) is a wide receiver for the New York Giants football team. Born in Paterson, he attended the University of Massachusetts. He holds the Giants' record for most receiving yards in a single season, 1,536 (1,405 m).

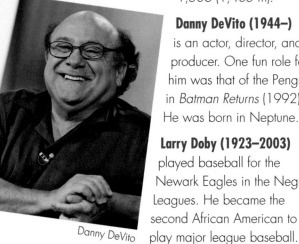
Danny DeVito

Danny DeVito (1944–) is an actor, director, and producer. One fun role for him was that of the Penguin in *Batman Returns* (1992). He was born in Neptune.

Larry Doby (1923–2003) played baseball for the Newark Eagles in the Negro Leagues. He became the second African American to play major league baseball. Born in South Carolina, he grew up in Paterson.

Mary Mapes Dodge (1831–1905), a longtime resident of Newark, was an author of children's books. She is best known for her children's classic, *Hans Brinker or The Silver Skates*.

Kirsten Dunst (1982–) is an actor who is known for her role as Mary Jane Watson in the Spider-Man movies. She was born in Point Pleasant.

Thomas Alva Edison (1847–1931) was an inventor who worked in West Orange. He invented the phonograph and the first practical electric light bulb.

Albert Einstein See page 77.

Jessie Fauset (1882–1961) was an African American poet and writer best known as the editor of the National Association for the Advancement of Colored People (NAACP) magazine, the *Crisis*, from 1919 to 1926. She wrote four novels, all of which feature the theme of race in America. She was born in Fredericksville.

Morris Frank See page 108.

George Gallup See page 103.

Althea Gibson (1927–2003) was one of the first African American women to play professional tennis. Born in South Carolina and raised in Harlem, she made New Jersey her home after retiring from the game. She won a total of 11 Grand Slam titles (singles and doubles) and later became the New Jersey state commissioner of athletics.

Althea Gibson

Kenneth Gibson See page 67.

Allen Ginsburg (1926–1997) was a leader among the "Beat Generation" of American poets that arose in the 1950s. His breakthrough poem "Howl" was published in 1955. He was born in Newark.

Frank "I Am the Law" Hague (1876–1956) was mayor of Jersey City from 1917 to 1947. He built a powerful political machine based on bribery and other corrupt practices.

William Frederick "Bull" Halsey (1882–1959) served as fleet admiral of the South Pacific forces during World War II. He was born in Elizabeth.

Alexander Hamilton See page 52.

Anne Hathaway (1982–) is a film actress who gained fame for her performance in *The Princess Diaries* in 2001. She went on to star in the box office hits *Valentine's Day* and *Alice in Wonderland*. Hathaway won an Academy Award, Golden Globe Award, and Screen Actors Guild Award for her performance in 2012's *Les Misérables*. She grew up in Milburn.

Lauryn Hill (1975–) is a Grammy Award–winning singer and music producer. Born in South Orange, she was a member of the band the Fugees.

Whitney Houston (1963–2012) was a popular singer and actor. One of her greatest hits was her 1992 release of Dolly Parton's "I Will Always Love You." Born in Newark, she was one of the biggest-selling artists in music history.

George Inness See page 11.

Wyclef Jean (1972–) is a Grammy Award–winning rapper, reggae artist, and producer. Born in Haiti, he moved to South Orange. He was a member of the band the Fugees.

Joyce Kilmer (1886–1918) was a poet and literary critic. Born in New Brunswick, he is best remembered for his poem "Trees."

Nathan Lane (1956–) is one of America's most famous Broadway and TV actors. He has also provided the voices for popular animated films such as *The Lion King* and *Stuart Little*. He was born in Jersey City.

Anne Morrow Lindbergh (1906–2001) was a pilot and author. One of her best-known books is *Gifts from the Sea*. Born in Englewood, she was married to aviator Charles Lindbergh and they lived in Hopewell for a number of years.

Effa Manley (1900–1981), a longtime resident of Newark, was the first woman elected to the Baseball Hall of Fame. With her co-ownership of the Newark Eagles, she became the only female team owner in the Negro Leagues.

Whitney Houston

Thomas Nast (1840–1902) was a political cartoonist. He was born in Germany, but lived in Morristown for many years.

Jack Nicholson (1937–) is an Academy Award–winning actor. He was born in Neptune and attended Manasquan High School.

Sam Patch See page 15.

William Paterson (1745–1806) was a signer of the United States Constitution. He was the second governor of New Jersey (1790–1793) and an associate justice of the U.S. Supreme Court (1793–1806).

Alice Paul See page 64.

Maria Pepe (1960–) was one of the first girls to play Little League baseball. She joined the Hoboken Little League in 1972, but was pressured to leave the team. Her case went to court, and in 1974 Little League softball was created for girls.

Molly Pitcher (1754–1832) got her nickname because she brought pitchers of water to soldiers during the Battle of Monmouth. Some say she also took over firing a cannon when her husband was wounded in battle. Her real name was Mary Ludwig Hays.

Queen Latifah (1970–) born in Newark, began her professional career as a rapper. She has gone on to be a film actress, model, TV and record producer, and talk show host. She has won numerous awards for her work, including a Golden Globe Award for Best Actress for the TV film *Life Support*.

James Lone Bear Revey See page 33.

Paul Robeson See page 65.

Washington Roebling (1837–1926) worked with his father, John Roebling, on the Brooklyn Bridge in New York. He was named the bridge's chief engineer when his father died, before the bridge was completed. Born in Pennsylvania, he served in the New Jersey militia during the Civil War.

Carl Sagan (1934–1996) was an astronomer and author whose TV programs and books opened up the world of science to millions of people around the world. Born in New York, he attended high school in Rahway. Sagan made numerous discoveries about space and the planets. He was inducted into the New Jersey Hall of Fame in 2009.

Antonin Scalia (1936–), born in Trenton, is a justice on the U.S. Supreme Court, appointed in 1986 by President Ronald Reagan. He is currently the longest-serving judge on the court and one of its most conservative thinkers.

Frank Sinatra (1915–1998) was a singer and actor. He was immensely popular as a singer in the 1940s, and his career continued into the 1990s. His role in the 1953 movie *From Here to Eternity* is considered a dramatic masterpiece. He was born in Hoboken.

Kevin Spacey (1959–) is an Academy Award–winning actor. He was born in South Orange.

Bruce Springsteen (1949–) was born in Freehold Borough and began his musical career in the nightclubs along Asbury Park's boardwalk. Many of his albums reflect his working-class New Jersey roots, including *Born to Run*, *Nebraska*, and *Born in the USA*.

John Lloyd Stephens (1805–1852) was an explorer and writer best known for his work on Maya civilization and in the planning of the Panama railroad in that country. He traveled widely throughout Central America exploring Maya ruins and was largely responsible for helping to "rediscover" the ancient civilization.

John Stevens (1749–1838), a longtime resident of Hoboken, was an engineer and inventor. He was a pioneer in the use of steam power, and he established a steam ferry from Hoboken to New York City. In 1825, he built the first American steam locomotive and demonstrated it on a short circular track in Hoboken. In 1830, he formed the Camden and Amboy Railroad and Transportation Company.

Jon Stewart (1962–) is an Emmy Award–winning comedian and producer who is best known for hosting *The Daily Show*. He grew up in Lawrence Township.

Martha Stewart (1941–) created a media empire that revolves around her interests in cooking and home remodeling. She grew up in Nutley.

James Still See page 56.

Meryl Streep (1949–) is a critically acclaimed actress of both stage and screen. She was born in Summit.

Meryl Streep

Walt Whitman

Samuel Sutphen See page 48.

Johnny Vander Meer (1914–1997) was the only professional baseball player in history to pitch two no-hitters in a row, which he did in 1938 while playing for the Cincinnati Reds. He was nicknamed the "Mad Dutchman." He was born in Prospect Park.

Christine Todd Whitman (1946–) grew up in Hunterdon County. She became New Jersey's first female governor in 1993. In 2001, President George W. Bush appointed her to head the Environmental Protection Agency (EPA), a position she held until 2003.

Walt Whitman (1819–1892) was a poet who lived in Camden during the last 19 years of his life. His masterpieces, including "When Lilacs Last in the Dooryard Bloom'd," "Song of Myself," and "Captain, My Captain," were published as part of his collection, *Leaves of Grass*.

William Carlos Williams See page 82.

Thomas Woodrow Wilson See page 92.

John Woolman See page 44.

Patience Lovell Wright (1725–1786) was a sculptor of portraits in wax. She was born in Bordentown.

RESOURCES

★ ★ ★

BOOKS

Nonfiction

Bryant, Jen. *A River of Words: The Story of William Carlos* Williams. Grand Rapids, Mich.: Eerdmans Publishing, 2008.

Cunningham, Kevin. *The New Jersey Colony*. New York: Children's Press, 2012.

Fritz, Jean. *Alexander Hamilton: The Outsider*. New York: G.P. Putnam's Sons, 2011.

Krull, Kathleen. *Albert Einstein*. New York: Viking, 2009.

Marsico, Katie. *Woodrow Wilson*. Tarrytown, N.Y.: Marshall Cavendish Benchmark, 2011.

Scholl, Elizabeth J. *New Jersey*. New York: Children's Press, 2008.

Fiction

Porter, Connie. *Addy's Summer Place*. Middleton, Wis.: American Girl, 2003.

Rinaldi, Ann. *Time Enough for Drums*. New York: Troll, 1988.

Ruby, Laura. *Lily's Ghosts*. New York: HarperCollins, 2003.

FACTS FOR NOW

Visit this Scholastic Web site for more information on New Jersey:
www.factsfornow.scholastic.com
Enter the keywords **New Jersey**

INDEX

★ ★ ★

AUTHOR'S TIPS AND SOURCE NOTES

★ ★ ★

Growing up in Little Falls, New Jersey, I heard lots of New Jersey lore and history. Writing this book gave me the chance to sort through the bits and pieces I remembered, and to fit those fragments into a bigger picture.

In the course of my research, I found many helpful and intriguing books and Web sites. *The WPA Guide to 1930s New Jersey*, although it was published in 1939, is still a wonderful resource on state history and folklore. *Words That Make New Jersey History: A Primary Source Reader*, edited by Howard L. Green, is a trove of firsthand accounts of New Jersey life from colonial times to the present. Another great resource is the *Encyclopedia of New Jersey*, edited by Maxine M. Luria and Marc Mappen.